J5

POLICY STUDIES IN EMPLOYMENT AND WELFARE NUMBER 38

General Editor: Sar A. Levitan

Disability and Work

The Economics of American Policy

Richard V. Burkhauser
and Robert H. Haveman

with the assistance of George Parsons

THE JOHNS HOPKINS UNIVERSITY PRESS
Baltimore and London

The Johns Hopkins University Press, Baltimore, Maryland 21218
The Johns Hopkins Press Ltd., London

Library of Congress Cataloging in Publication Data

Burkhauser, Richard V.
  Disability and work.

  (Policy studies in employment and welfare; no. 38)
  Bibliography: p. 123
  Includes index.
  1. Handicapped—Employment—United States.
I. Haveman, Robert H.   II. Parsons, George.
III. Title.   IV. Series.
HD7256.U5B87   331.5'9'0973   82-113
ISBN 0-8018-2834-1   AACR2

Contents

List of Tables

Disability and Work

disincentives
microcosm
equity

1
Introduction

Political currents during the early 1980s have challenged the role of the federal government in American society. The implications of that challenge have emerged in terms of specific proposals that would fundamentally change the direction of public policy. The structure and magnitude of social insurance and social welfare programs that have so greatly reduced poverty over the last twenty years are being reconsidered to see whether the programs comprise the most efficient and equitable means of providing protection and social adequacy. The evaluation is spurred by a sense that, while poverty has been significantly reduced, the costs imposed by the disincentives and regulations implicit in these programs and the taxes required to finance them are greater than necessary to provide a socially acceptable safety net. These costs, as we will see, involve real efficiency losses in the form of reduced work, productivity, and savings.

No set of programs offers a better microcosm of the political, moral, and economic debates that will result from this general rethinking of the role of social policy than those comprising the U.S. disability system. A teenager born with cerebral palsy, a young worker injured on the job, a middle-aged executive who suffers a heart attack at home, a wheelchair-bound veteran with service-related health problems, or an unemployed older worker with diminished strength and abilities may all have difficulty working and thus are possible clients of our disability system. Clearly, a strong moral commitment to provide some form of protection and compensation to such people exists in this country. However, in-

1

creases in public spending on programs for the disabled and the network of regulations established in an attempt to integrate fully the handicapped into society have caused even the traditional supporters of government intervention to pause. Concern with the rising costs of disability programs has affected all recent administrations, irrespective of political party.

Any informed debate over the direction of U.S. disability policy must take into account the complex nature of the existing system—its size, structure, recent growth, economic status, and labor market effects. It is the purpose of this volume to provide the background necessary to comprehend the ramifications of the proposed changes in policy. It is only through understanding the current rationale and workings of disability policy and its accomplishments and failures that proposed policy measures based on a changed rationale can be evaluated.

In this volume we present a comprehensive description of the large number of public programs targeted on workers—largely older workers—with some identifiable health problem. We refer to this set of programs as *U.S. disability policy.* These numerous programs are interrelated in complicated ways, they are costly, and they are growing rapidly. The structure and magnitude of this set of programs have a substantial effect on the economic status of older workers, their work effort, and their labor market participation. Our discussion describes the nature of current disability policy and attempts to marshal the available research findings on the magnitude of these welfare and labor market effects.

As expected, the evidence on labor supply and program effectiveness is not precise and is often circumstantial. The evidence does suggest that disability policy substantially improves the economic status of impaired workers and their families, even though these workers remain relatively poor with these programs in place. The income support provided by these programs also tends to reduce work incentives for this population. The decrease in work effort attributable to disability income support programs accounts for some of the observed decline in labor force participation and work effort among older males. At least some of the "early retirement" puzzle is thereby explained. These work disincentives also undermine the success of training and rehabilitation efforts and account for the low percentage of transfer recipients who leave the benefit roles for regular employment.

Therefore this volume is a background volume, and not a research volume. Its value is in its comprehensive view of the nature and impacts of the system which comprises U.S. disability policy, and not in its presentation of new research results or proposals. By drawing on the existing body of research, the volume does contribute to the shape of the debate on new directions for disability policy. It does not lead, however, to any conclusions concerning whether the system should be more redistributive and less like insurance, or whether public policies designed to stimulate the employment of disabled workers, reduce effective replacement rates, or guarantee equal access to mobility and public facilities are desirable. Clearly some programs are more costly than others, and the strength of one's commitment to a given level of income adequacy or equal access will influence judgment as to the value of various program features. However, regardless of one's position, the information provided by this volume will be of value. Any participant in the policy debate will at least be able to see the costs and benefits of his or her current commitment.

In addition to providing background on the structure and impacts of U.S. disability policy, the volume contributes to a fuller understanding of a recent phenomenon with important policy implications—the rapid decline in the labor force participation and work effort of older male workers. During the last decade the supply of male workers older than 45 but younger than 65 years has fallen dramatically. While 95 percent of male workers aged 45 to 54 were in the labor force in 1968, only 84 percent of them were supplying labor in 1978. Similarly, 84 percent of male workers aged 55 to 64 were in the labor force in 1968; only 74 percent were there in 1978. Social Security retirement benefits have been available and have been gaining in value for male workers aged 62 to 65 since 1961, and an increasing proportion of these workers have been accepting benefits and retiring from the work force. In 1978, 51 percent of male workers between 62 and 65 years of age were receiving Social Security retirement or disability benefits. Coincidentally, from 1961 to 1978 the labor force participation of this group fell from just over 4 in 5 to less than 3 in 5.

Although Social Security retirement benefits are not available for workers younger than 62, other sources of nonwork income support are available to them, and on increasingly generous terms. The two primary sources of support are private retirement pensions and disability income transfers. Over the past decade these sources of nonwork income—like the Social Security early retirement provision—have grown rapidly.

Consider, first, the private retirement pension option. While only about 20 percent of employees were covered by pension plans with early retirement provisions in 1962, by the early 1970s over 90 percent were so covered.[1] Moreover, during the last decade, control over early retirement decisions under such plans has increasingly switched from the manager's approval to the worker's discretion. As a result of these trends, the number of private pension recipients increased from 0.5 million in 1950 to over 7 million in the late 1970s. A substantial share of this enormous increase is due to economic incentives that influence individuals to retire prior to age 65.

Income from disability programs has also supported retirement from the work force for a rapidly growing number of workers with some recognizable physical or mental impairment. For example, in 1968 the Social Security Disability Insurance program (SSDI) provided income support to 1.3 million workers; by 1978 this figure had more than doubled, to 2.9 million. All of these recipients—over 2.2 percent of the work force in 1978—were younger than 65 years of age. In addition to SSDI, there are several other major disability-related transfer programs—Supplemental Security Income (SSI), Veterans' Compensation, Workers' Compensation, and the Black Lung program—all of which support working-age individuals. Indeed, several dozen programs that provide assistance to disabled working-age people can be identified in the U.S. government budget. This constellation of programs provides support that makes retirement from the active labor force easier than otherwise, and this contributes to the "early retirement" phenomenon.

This volume deals with this system of disability-related income support programs and other programs targeted on disabled workers. In it, we attempt to understand the nature of this large collection of public provisions for disabled people, and how it has come to absorb nearly $70 billion—10 percent of total public expenditures. More importantly, we attempt to appraise the economic effects of these policies and to identify the major issues underlying the ongoing debate over disability policy, including the contribution of these programs to the decline in the labor force participation of older male workers.

The study has five substantive chapters. In Chapter 2 we describe the disabled working-age population[2] on which the analysis focuses, and inquire into the rationale put forward to explain the substantial government intervention on their behalf. The data suggest that about 17 percent of the working-age (ages 18 to 64) population have some degree of impairment, and about one-half of this impaired population are severely disabled. This disabled population is concentrated in the older age categories, in the black population, and in the groups with less education. Moreover, the disabled population is less likely to be married and more likely to live on a farm or in a rural area than is the population without impairments. Finally, the disabled work far less than the nondisabled, and they have far less income.

This group of citizens has been the focus of major public programs. Some provide income support, others compensate for the loss of work capacity due to injuries, others provide medical care and training and rehabilitation services, and still others seek to stimulate the employment demand for these workers. Most recently, government has accepted the goal of "equal access" to education, employment, and mobility for disabled people and has sought to implement it through regulations imposed on both private sector businesses and public agencies. Important questions arise: Why and to what degree should the public sector—the federal government in particular—engage in these activities? Is the public intervention based on efficiency principles, or is it justified largely on equity and humanitarian grounds? Chapter 2 explores these questions and seeks to set forth the rationale for collective action in this area.

In Chapter 3 we provide an overview of the large and complex set of programs providing assistance or services to disabled workers. These programs range from the large and established Social Security Disability Insurance (SSDI) program to newer income support programs such as the Black Lung program, to training and rehabilitation programs, to new "affirmative action" efforts to assure equal opportunity for handicapped workers in employment and mobility. The centerpiece of this chapter is a large matrix that identifies the primary programs and displays a number of their important economic characteristics. This discussion conveys the far-reaching nature of U.S. policy toward disabled workers, and emphasizes the rapid growth in these programs—in terms of both public expenditures and number of recipients—during the 1970s.

Chapter 4 discusses the primary issues surrounding income support policies toward disabled workers. Nearly all of these issues concern the impact of the set of disability programs on the economic status and labor market activity of disabled people. Clearly the rapid growth in expenditures on these programs is one indicator of the extent to which the income and other needs of the disabled are being served by public policy. We inquire into the causes of this program growth and find that a substantial increase in the rate at which these programs replace income lost from impairment is an important determinant. These high replacement rates imply a loss of work incentives. This labor supply effect has been studied from a number of vantage points, and we describe and critique these research findings. Finally, we review some of the administrative problems that plague disability income support policy, many of them inherent in the large number of overlapping and nonintegrated programs which comprise this policy.

Offsetting to some extent the work disincentives implicit in the income support programs are activities providing rehabilitation and training services to handicapped workers and programs seeking to create jobs for them. In Chapter 5 we examine the available evidence on the extent to which these labor market activities yield benefits in excess of their costs. The programs on which we focus are the vocational rehabilitation program, the nation's system of sheltered workshops, and the newer policy initiatives of direct job creation and regulations to assure equal access. Because the history of these latter programs is so short, our evaluative comments on them must, of necessity, be brief.

Finally, in Chapter 6, we address a few of the fundamental issues surrounding disability policy. These involve the conflict between the insurance and redistribution goals of disability policy, the role of disability in general employment policy (including the appropriate role of employment generation efforts for handicapped people), and the merits and limitations of "equal access" efforts. These issues underlie the current public debate over the directions for change in disability policy.

2

The Working-Age Disabled: Who Are They and Why Should They Be Helped?

The Size of the
Working-Age Disabled Population

In 1978 there were 127 million U.S. citizens between the ages of 18 and 64. This is the group commonly thought of as the working-age population, though at any given time a large number of them will be neither working nor looking for work. For example, in 1978 about 24 million of the total, or nearly 20 percent, were not in the labor force, and another 5 million were unemployed. Some of the 127 million are young people who are attending college full time or are engaged in some other form of postsecondary education or training. Some choose not to be in the labor force because of a preference for engaging in child care, volunteer activities, or home work responsibilities. Some of them are retired with the support of pensions or another non-labor-market income.

But some of the 127 million people in the working-age population are not in the labor force because of a health problem or a handicap. The appropriateness of this disabled working-age population as the target of disability policy can be appraised by comparing the demographic and economic characteristics of its members with those of the nondisabled population.

A definition of *disablement* or *impairment* is necessary to identify the working-age disabled population. Unfortunately, there is no definition

7

that is unambiguously the correct one, as the concept of disability ultimately rests on a social judgment. Only when a person falls significantly below some threshold of deviation from the average does society designate that person as sufficiently atypical to warrant special attention. When the characteristic at stake is the physical or mental capacity of a person to engage in productive activities, that person is considered handicapped or disabled. However, society does not unambiguously reveal who is so designated. Defining the disabled population therefore requires reliance on a surrogate or proxy.

One purpose of this discussion is to investigate the relationship between disability and labor market activity. As a result, the definition of *disability* that is most appropriate here is one that focuses on the work-related aspects of impairments and that thereby makes the tie between disablement and work effort explicit. The following definition of *impairment* is consistent with this concept: a limitation of a physical, mental, or emotional sort which reduces, to varying degrees, one's ability to perform the functions required for jobs one is, on other grounds, qualified to hold. This definition captures the three aspects of an impairment which are important in determining its effect on a person's ability to function effectively in the labor market. These are: the extent to which the person is limited in specific work-related functions, the severity of these limitations, and the requirements in terms of functional performance which are imposed by a person's occupation.

This definition could be based on a quantitative specification of the loss of permanent earnings capacity attributable to mental or physical impairments associated with various degrees of disablement. Such a definition would require medical examinations of an extensive national sample of individuals and an evaluation of any recorded earnings capacity shortfall. An estimate based on such a definition would be ideal; unfortunately, such a survey has not been undertaken in the United States, and the required data are not available. In estimating the extent of disability in the working-age population we are forced, therefore, to substitute definitions that are available and that have been used in making disability determinations.

In describing the disabled, we are limited to survey data that use a definition of disability based on self-evaluation. In this alternative, a person is provided with a definition of disability and a set of work-related degrees of impairment consistent with this definition, and then asked to

Table 2.1. Working-Age Disabled Population by Severity of Disability, 1978

	Estimated Number of Persons (millions)	Percentage of Total Population Aged 18 to 64	Percentage of Disabled
Severely disabled	10.8	8.5	50.7
Occupationally disabled	4.7	3.7	22.1
With secondary work limitations	5.8	4.6	27.2
Total	21.3	16.8	100.0

SOURCE: Social Security Administration's Survey of Disability and Work, 1978.

classify him/herself appropriately. Clearly, such a self-evaulation measure entails numerous problems. For example, because people are evaluating their own health, they may give excessive weight to acute or transitory illnesses. Moreover, persons who are receiving income support from some disability program are likely to state that their health is poor. Finally, such a measure, precisely because it is subjective, will introduce biases depending on whether the person is a worrier or an optimist, one who has chronic or only temporary problems, and/or one who has a long or a short history of work.

The most complete surveys of the extent of the disabled working-age population come from data collected by the Social Security Administration (SSA) which relies on household interviews in which individuals are asked to classify themselves in terms of the extensiveness of impairment.[1] Table 2.1 provides an estimate of the current extent of disability based on self-reported information from the 1978 Social Security Survey of Disability and Work. In 1978 the disabled working-age population is estimated to have been 21 million people. Hence, approximately 17 percent of the total working-age population of 127 million had some degree of self-perceived impairment. In table 2.1 this total is broken down into three classes of severity. Over one-half of the population that is self-classified as disabled stipulate the presence of a severe disability, one that eliminates the possibility of working regularly or at all. Nearly one-quarter state that their impairment has forced a change in occupation or has limited them to less than full-time work.

This number of disabled people is large, especially in comparison with the total number of working-age people who are not in the labor force. As indicated, only about 24 million working-age people were not in the labor

Table 2.2 Composition of Disabled Working-Age Population, 1978
(In Thousands)

Characteristic	Total Population	Severely Disabled	Disabled, but Not Severely*	Not Disabled
Total population	127,086	10,771	10,519	105,796
Race				
White	111,212	8,818	9,256	93,138
Nonwhite	15,212	1,953	1,263	12,657
Sex				
Male	63,120	4,610	5,339	53,171
Female	63,966	6,161	5,180	52,625
Age				
18 to 34	58,213	1,485	3,215	53,513
35 to 44	24,887	1,585	2,016	21,286
45 to 54	23,681	2,670	2,915	18,095
55 to 64	20,305	5,031	2,372	12,901
Marital Status				
Married	86,333	6,777	7,571	71,984
Widowed	3,675	1,121	253	2,301
Divorced, separated	10,927	1,673	1,170	8,084
Never married	26,004	1,195	1,524	23,285
Education				
8 years or fewer	14,619	3,622	1,609	9,388
High school	68,354	5,697	6,006	56,651
College	43,524	1,382	2,826	39,316

SOURCE: Social Security Administration's Survey of Disability and Work, 1978.
*Includes occupationally disabled and disabled with secondary work limitations.

force in 1978. Given the large number of these nonworkers who were nonemployed women, students, or early retirees, it must follow that a high proportion of people who report themselves as disabled are simultaneously in the labor force and employed. This, as we will see, is the case.

The Demographic Composition
of the Working-Age Disabled Population

The demographic composition of the population of disabled working-age people is not unexpected (see table 2.2). The group of disabled (regardless of the degree of disability) contains relatively more blacks and other minorities than does the rest of the population. Moreover, this group is less educated, employed in lower-paying occupations, less frequently employed, and earning less than the remainder of the population.

Disability is more prevalent among women than among men (see table 2.2; 17.7 percent of women had some degree of disability compared to 15.8 percent of men), with the disparity even greater between men and women who classify themselves as severely disabled. The composition of the disabled is also heavily weighted toward older people. While 35 percent of the working-age population were at least 45 years old, 71 percent of the severely disabled population were older than 45. Indeed, 47 percent of the severely disabled group were older than 55 years. This is reflected in the median ages of the severely disabled and the nondisabled—the median age of the former group is 15 years greater than that of the latter.

The data for 1978 also show that blacks and other nonwhites are more heavily represented among the disabled than among the general working-age population. While nonwhites composed 12 percent of the total working-age population, they accounted for 15 percent of the disabled population and over 18 percent of the severely disabled population. Although the data in table 2.2 do not indicate it, disabled blacks had a lower median age than disabled whites.

The composition of the disabled population is heavily weighted toward individuals with low educational attainment. While only 9 percent of the nondisabled population had 8 or fewer years of education, approximately 34 percent of the severely disabled group had not attended high school. Of course part of this compositional effect is explained by the relationship between age and disability, as older people also tend to be less educated.[2]

Finally, the disabled population—in particular, the severely disabled group—is composed of unmarried individuals to a larger extent than is the nondisabled population. While about 68 percent of the nondisabled population are married, only about 63 percent of the severely disabled are married. Consistent with this pattern, the disabled population is more heavily composed of divorced and widowed individuals than is the nondisabled population. The high concentration of widows or widowers among the disabled is largely explained by the older average age among the disabled group.

An alternative way of looking at the distribution of disability among the working-age population is to see how likely it is to find a disabled person chosen at random from various population groups. This conditional probability pattern is displayed in table 2.3. This table shows that

Table 2.3 Conditional Probability of Disability within the Working-Age Population Given Different Demographic Characteristics, 1978

Characteristic	Given the Characteristic, the Probability of Being:		
	Severely Disabled	Disabled, but Not Severely	Not Disabled
Total working-age population	.08	.08	.84
Nonwhite	.12	.08	.80
Fifty-five years old or older	.25	.12	.63
Eight years of schooling or fewer	.25	.11	.64

SOURCE: Derived from table 2.2. (Social Security Administration's Survey of Disability and Work, 1978.)

if a random draw were made from the total working-age population, the chance of obtaining a severely disabled person would be 8 percent. However, if one were to make a random draw from the nonwhite working-age population, the chance of obtaining a severely disabled person would be 12 percent. The chances increase if one were to make a random draw from the working-age population that is either 55 years old or more or that has 8 or fewer years of school. For the group of older workers, the chance of drawing a severely disabled person is 25 percent; for working-age people with little education, the chance of drawing a severely disabled person is also 25 percent. For these last two categories, the probability of drawing someone who is severely disabled is three times as large as in the working-age population as a whole.[3]

The Economic Status
of the Disabled Working-Age Population

Consistent with economic theory, the wage earnings of two individuals with the same nonwage income and tastes for work will differ depending upon the productivity of the two individuals as perceived by employers. Productivity, in turn, depends on a host of other characteristics of the individual: education, age, sex, job experience, and so on. In addition to productivity, other factors can also influence individual earnings. For example, labor market discrimination may make it more difficult for black individuals than for white individuals to obtain and keep jobs, or to move up internal job ladders.

Leaving aside considerations of health status, we have observed that the disabled have productivity characteristics that would imply relatively low earnings. Disabled people tend to be older workers, and they tend to be workers with relatively low levels of education. In addition, because the disabled population has a disproportionate share of women and blacks, discrimination in the labor market may tend to constrain their realized earnings. As a result, even without health problems disabled adults would tend to have earnings below those of the working-age population.

By definition, however, disabled individuals do have health problems, although in varying degrees of severity. As a result, observed earnings for them are likely to be even lower than would be expected from their adverse demographic and economic characteristics. In some sense, then, they are "doubly disadvantaged" in their expected labor market performance.

Labor market performance is itself an inadequate indicator of economic status for both the nondisabled and the disabled. Cash transfers are large and have been growing rapidly, and these have surely both raised measured economic status for all groups and closed the gap between the disabled and the nondisabled. Moreover, in the 1970s, in-kind transfers have shown rapid increases—especially in the areas of food, medical care, and housing—and these, too, have both raised measured status and decreased the gap between the disabled and the nondisabled. If these differences were recognized, and perhaps asset differences as well, the economic status of the disabled—both absolute and relative—would appear different from a picture based on earnings alone.[4]

Table 2.4 presents some evidence on the labor market performance of workers with different disability levels. The income data are based on 1972 estimates and are adjusted to 1978 dollars. As compared to the nondisabled working-age population, the severely disabled population is heavily underrepresented in the labor force. Roughly 82 percent of nondisabled persons are participants in the labor force, compared to 13 percent of the severely disabled. Those who are not severely disabled, however, display labor force participation characteristics similar to those without disablement. For the employed population, substantial differences between the disabled and nondisabled populations also exist. Whereas 86 percent of the nondisabled employed population work full time, only 51 percent of the severely disabled employed are full-time

Table 2.4 Labor Force Characteristics of the Disabled

Characteristic	Total Population	Severely Disabled	Disabled, but Not Severely	Not Disabled
Labor force status, 1973 (1978)*				
Not in labor force	26.8% (19.2%)	81.8% (65.8%)	22.5% (17.9%)	22.5% (14.5%)
Employed full time	56.1% (61.6%)	5.7% (6.0%)	52.8% (55.8%)	60.6% (67.9%)
Employed part time	12.2% (10.8%)	8.1% (5.8%)	18.4% (16.0%)	12.0% (10.7%)
Unemployed	3.7% (3.6%)	3.4% (1.5%)	5.7% (4.7%)	3.7% (3.7%)
Weekly wage and salary earnings, 1972 (in 1978 dollars)†				
Less than $78	7.9%	32.3%	14.9%	7.0%
$78 to $154	17.2%	19.1%	20.6%	16.9%
$155 to $310	41.3%	14.3%	40.0%	41.9%
$310 or more	27.6%	11.6%	18.4%	28.7%
Not reported	5.9%	22.7%	6.2%	5.6%
Median weekly earnings	$226	$101	$187	$229
Median annual earnings	$10,418	$3,602	$8,354	$10,783

SOURCES: 1972 Data: Lando and Knute (1976), p. 7.
1978 Data: Social Security Administration's Survey of Disability and Work, 1978. (These are preliminary data obtained from the Social Security Administration.)

NOTE: Percentages may not sum to 100 due to incomplete reporting of labor force status and rounding error.

*Numbers given in parentheses are for 1978; these were the only available data on labor force characteristics in 1978.

† Weekly earnings and median annual earnings are inflated to 1978 from 1972 data using the Consumer Price Index, all items. The data on earnings excludes those not in the labor force.

workers. In terms of the distinction between full- and part-time work, the not-severely-disabled group lies between the severely disabled and non-disabled groups, but resembles the latter group more closely than the former.

The weekly earnings statistics are most revealing regarding economic status. In 1972 only 7 percent of the nondisabled population earned less than $78 (in 1978 dollars) per week. However, nearly one-third of the severely disabled population had such low earnings.[5] While some fraction of this differential is no doubt due to the higher incidence of part-time work and nonwork of the severely disabled, a substantial portion is due to wage rate differentials between the two groups. This disparity is reflected partially in the median annual earnings data presented in the last line of table 2.4. The median for the severely disabled ($3,602 in 1978 dollars) is about one-third of that for the nondisabled ($10,783 in 1978 dollars). As in the case of labor force participation, the earnings pattern of those who are not severely disabled more closely resembles that of the nondisabled population than that of the severely disabled population.

In terms of labor market performance, then, the disabled—especially the severely disabled—are at a serious disadvantage relative to the nondisabled. They work fewer hours per year and at lower-paying jobs than the nondisabled and, as a consequence, earn far less than do the nondisabled. Generally the severely disabled earn only about one-third of the income of the nondisabled, while the not severely disabled have wage earnings of about two-thirds of the income of the nondisabled population. The not-severely-disabled population appears to be substantially different from the severely disabled group, in many ways more closely resembling the nondisabled population than it does the severely disabled population. Moreover, as hinted at earlier, the severely disabled population is not without earnings or employment and, as will be seen, a substantial share of their total income is from labor market activity.

These data address only the labor market performance of the disabled and the nondisabled. A more accurate picture of economic status is obtained by looking at the total income of the living unit of disabled people.[6] This total income includes wage earnings, income from public and private transfer programs, and income such as interest, dividends, and rent. Because of their loss of wage earnings or of the ability to earn, disabled individuals are often eligible for a number of transfer benefits.

Table 2.5 Estimated Median Family Income and Poverty Incidence of the Disabled and Nondisabled, by Marital Status

Category	Total Population:		Severely Disabled:		Disabled, but Not Severely:		Not Disabled:	
	Median Income in 1978	Poverty Incidence in 1972	Median Income in 1978	Poverty Incidence in 1972	Median Income in 1978	Poverty Incidence in 1972	Median Income in 1978	Poverty Incidence in 1972
Total	$16,425	11.9(12.1)*	$ 9,128	37.4 (25.1)	$14,000	14.8 (10.7)	$17,246	9.5 (11.0)
Married†	$18,602	6.7	$13,965	23.2	$16,664	9.1	$19,155	5.4
Single†	$ 7,450	29.7	$ 3,449	65.3	$ 6,546	30.9	$ 8,373	24.9

SOURCES: 1972 Data: Lando and Krute (1976), p. 9. 1978 Data: Social Security Administration's Survey of Disability and Work, 1978. (These are preliminary data obtained from the Social Security Administration.) Weights for married and single data: Allan (1976), p. 25.

NOTE: Only *total* median family income for each disability status group is actual 1978 data (first row in this table). The proportion of median family income in each category (married and single) to total median income within the disability status group is assumed to be the same as found in 1972. Family income data must be interpreted with care. See Note 8 to chapter 2.

*Figures given in parentheses are for 1978.

† Data for these two categories (married and single) are calculated as weighted averages of the median income and poverty incidence of men and women within these categories. The weights are the proportion of men and proportion of women to total number of persons in each category. Such a transformation will not produce the true median family income for each category, but it does provide a reasonable estimate.

These benefits tend to replace income "lost" due to disablement. Once again looking at data from the 1978 Social Security Survey of Disability and Work, we find that while wage income accounts for 90 percent of total income for the living units of the nondisabled, it contributes only 59 percent of the income of households with a severely disabled working-age adult.[7] Conversely, public and private income support programs contribute a substantially larger share of the total income of the severely disabled than of the nondisabled. Indeed, income support payments account for about 30 percent of household income for the severely disabled, as compared to less than 5 percent for the nondisabled. Once again, the severely disabled make up a population that differs greatly from the remainder of the disabled. Those in the latter group are far less reliant on income transfers—and more reliant on earnings—than are the severely disabled. The pattern of income sources for the not severely disabled more closely resembles that of the nondisabled than that of the severely disabled.

Table 2.5 compares the median household income and poverty incidences of the disabled and the nondisabled, adjusted for marital status, within each category. Once again the most striking distinction is between the severely disabled and all other people, either not disabled or disabled but not severely. The severely disabled—even with income transfers and spouse's earnings—have only 53 percent of the income of the nondisabled, although this disparity is substantially less for the severely disabled who are married. The income of these living units is 73 percent of the family incomes of married couples who are not disabled. For the nonmarried, however, the gap is much larger. Single severely disabled people have only about 41 percent of the income of their nondisabled counterparts. The not severely disabled lie about halfway between the severely disabled and the nondisabled in terms of total income. While the wage and salary income of the not severely disabled was closer to that of the nondisabled group than to that of the severely disabled, the receipt of greater amounts of transfer income by the severely disabled closes this relative gap among the groups. The enormity of the remaining gap among the groups should not be neglected, however.[8]

The remaining income disparity and the low absolute median income level of the disabled imply a substantial difference in the incidence of poverty among the groups.[9] In 1978, while 11 percent of the nondisabled population was classified as being income poor, 25 percent of the severely disabled group was in poverty. The not severely disabled have a poverty incidence comparable to that of the nondisabled population. The degree of poverty incidence among the disabled is shown to have declined substantially between 1972 and 1978.

This brief sketch of the characteristics of the group of disabled working-age people is a necessary first step to understanding the nature of public policy toward the disabled population and assessing proposals for the revision of this policy. However, before looking at what it is that government does on behalf of the disabled, we would do well to step back and ask why government intervenes at all in support of this group. As we will see, several rationales for government intervention have been offered.

Why Should the Government
Share the Cost of Disability?

Three primary rationales have been offered in support of government policy in the disability area. The first adopts a standard economic perspective and develops the general case for government intervention in this area. This "neoclassical" approach applies primarily to income support interventions or traditional labor supply side measures such as job training and rehabilitation. From it, an economic rationale for policy of the sort undertaken until the mid-1970s can be discerned. However, as we shall see, the late 1970s witnessed a nontraditional intervention into the market—the attempt to create jobs directly for handicapped and other disadvantaged workers, such as the unskilled and those with little education. This intervention supplements the traditional approaches and rests on a quite different economic rationale, our second one. The third rational involves what could be called a "radical" program of government intervention—the decision to accommodate the presence of handicapped citizens by causing changes in social and economic arrangements designed to guarantee the disabled "equal access" to employment, education, and mobility.

Sharing and Reducing Disability Costs:
The Standard Rationale

The presence of an impairment that affects a person's ability to function normally either at home or in the work force results in a fall in

18

aggregate social welfare. This reduction in aggregate welfare is appropriately viewed as a social cost.

If neither society nor the impaired person's family is affected by the individual's impairment or takes action in response to it, the full cost of the handicap falls on the disabled person. These costs take a variety of forms including: (1) medical care costs; (2) the loss of labor market earnings and other sources of productivity; (3) the cost of special aids (appliances, nurses, assistants) required for performing standard (or, in some cases, minimal) daily functions; and (4) the loss of social and psychological well-being—all attributable to the impairment. More realistically, however, the costs are not all private. Rather, both society at large and the impaired person's family suffer some loss of well-being, that is, they incur a real cost as the result of the impairment. This cost can result from legal obligations to provide financially for a disabled worker or simply because of a felt moral or ethical responsibility to the impaired individual. These losses are, in effect, what economists define as negative externalities or spillovers. They occur when the actions of a single individual affect the well-being of others. Their presence provides a clue to why government intervenes to share or reduce the costs of disability.

When no private agreements exist by which compensation can pass when such spillovers exist to force individuals to bear the full cost of their behavior, then the private costs they bear only partially reflect true social cost. As a result, their decisions are likely to be erroneous ones; they may be right for themselves, but they are surely wrong from society's point of view. For example, when the costs of a potential impairment are only partially borne by an individual, he or she is likely to take fewer precautions than optimal socially to avoid that impairment. Collective action is required to correct such erroneous signals; in the economist's jargon, it is necessary to "internalize externalities."

A second "neo-classical" rationale for cost-sharing or cost-reducing collective action is also related to the existence of an externality, but the source of the spillover is somewhat different in this case. Individuals in society may experience "collective compassion" costs because of the loss of well-being of people with handicaps. As a result, these individuals are likely to be willing to contribute something, however small, to the well-being of an impaired individual. While the option of individual charity may be open to them, the amount such individuals are willing to contribute is likely to depend on the existence of contributions by others.

The optimal level can be achieved only when all beneficiaries of the reduction in "collective compassion" costs are contributing. Again, there is a potential role for public sector intervention.

A third standard "neo-classical" economic rationale for collective action stems from the same externality. Consider, for example, the provision of rehabilitation services, appliances, or job retraining services. These activities have all the characteristics of an investment. Because of both constraints on the ability of a disabled person to finance these investments[10] and the fact that some benefits of these investments spillover onto individuals other than the impaired person, the level of investment that would be undertaken voluntarily is likely to be less than optimal. Again, collective action, presumably in the form of public sector policy, is required in order to achieve an efficient level of investment in activities to reduce the costs of disability.

A final potential role for public sector efforts to share or reduce disability costs stems from a purely equity or humanitarian motive. Even with optimal, efficiency-based collective action, disabled individuals may be at the bottom of the income distribution. In this case, income support for disabled people may convey social benefits, but the benefits in this case stem from income redistribution goals rather than any disability-related characteristics of the beneficiaries. Again, government intervention is necessary to accomplish such redistribution.[11]

These four "neo-classical" economic-based rationales—three rooted in efficiency considerations and one related to an equity goal—form the case for public cost-sharing or cost-reducing interventions when aggregate disability costs exist. It could, however, be claimed that other institutions—namely, private insurance markets or the legal system—could satisfy at least some of these functions, hence reducing or eliminating the need for public sector action. For several reasons, however, these institutions would appear to be deficient.

For one thing, the conditions necessary for the private insurance market to work adequately do not exist. Insurance markets for disability coverage are both partial and seriously deficient. Indeed, coverage for the full private costs of disablement—including social and psychological costs—is generally unavailable. In addition, given the external effects of impairments described here, even a fully informed individual operating in a perfect insurance market would not purchase the optimal level of insurance coverage. Hence, while the existence of private disability insurance markets does blunt the four bases for collective action, it apparently does not eliminate them.

The legal system does not appear to be able to serve these functions either. While it is possible to conceptualize the award of full compensation of private disability costs in cases where legal liability is determined, in practice the number of such cases relative to the total volume of impairments does not appear to be large. Moreover, as many legal scholars point out, the legal system is not equipped to assign damages efficiently, and in fact does so in relatively few cases. Again, this possibility—like the private insurance possibility—would not seem to fully offset the case for public intervention based on the four rationales discussed previously.

Based on these rationales for collective intervention, government policy in the disability area would appear to have two primary functions: establishing mechanisms to achieve the appropriate *sharing* of the costs of impairments and sponsoring programs to achieve an optimal *reduction* in the aggregate cost of disability.

In performing these functions, public intervention can clearly take a wide variety of forms. At one extreme, the public sector could simply attempt to create a more comprehensive and accessible private insurance market for disability. Alternatively, to insure comprehensive coverage, the government could establish its own insurance system, a social insurance system. The choice, ultimately, rests on an appraisal of the costs associated with each approach—an assessment of the resource allocation efficiency of each approach.

An alternative approach, though complementary to social disability insurance, would recognize that for some impairments liability should fall on a specific group. The most common variant of this approach provides compensation at some level for impairments experienced on the job, with liability for financing falling on employers. Such an approach (commonly referred to as workers' compensation) contributes to the cost-sharing objective and simultaneously provides employers with incentives to undertake actions that will reduce the number of impairments and the associated costs of disability.[12]

Actions taken after an impairment has occurred can also reduce the aggregate cost of disability. The provisions of job training or skill training or of rehabilitation services are examples of such actions. These interventions, it should be noted, have the character of standard public investments, and their effectiveness can be judged with the help of benefit-cost analysis techniques.

These cost-sharing and cost-reducing options, then, form the menu of potential public sector interventions designed to correct the externalities and other efficiency considerations surrounding disability, and to achieve equity goals. Choice among these options must ultimately be a social one, a choice resting on a variety of considerations: the level of costs related to handicaps; the breakdown of these costs among those impaired and other citizens affected by impairments; the extent to which nonimpaired citizens wish to undertake compensation of the direct costs of disability; assessment of the feasibility, administrative costs, and incentive effects of the various options; and the tastes of members of society for providing assistance to those among the disabled population with the lowest incomes. Many of these considerations reflect social judgments and tastes and have but a small chance of being objectively appraised by standard welfare criteria. Ultimately, in a democratic society, leaders designated to reflect somehow these social tastes and to reconcile competing interests must choose a system of public interventions in the disability area designed to fulfill the economic rationale for such policy measures and to achieve both cost-sharing and cost-reduction goals.

Direct Labor Market Interventions: A "Second Best" Rationale

From a discussion of equity and efficiency considerations based on a standard "neo-classical" economic rationale for income support programs or traditional supply-side interventions through job training and rehabilitation, we turn to a discussion of the economic rationale for the relatively new government interventions in the market designed to create jobs for disadvantaged workers. These interventions—all of which we refer to as direct job creation—include employment subsidies for disabled workers, the subsidization of enterprises established for the purpose of employing handicapped workers (for example, sheltered workshops), the subsidization of work-place adaptation costs, the imposition of quotas for the hiring of disabled workers on individual enterprises, or the provision of public employment.

What, then, is the economic rationale for such direct job creation efforts? This rationale starts from a perception of the adverse economic effects of existing legal and institutional constraints on the operation of the labor market. Because of these constraints—minimum wage laws, government regulation of the work place, employer discriminatory behavior, union power and influence, supply disincentives caused by income transfer and income and payroll tax programs, and demand disincentives caused by unemployment insurance and payroll taxes—labor markets do not respond quickly to changes in labor supply or demand, and a wedge is created between the gross wage paid by employers and the net wage received by workers. Employer-borne gross wage costs are increased relative to the perceived marginal product of low-skilled workers, and the net wage received by workers is reduced relative to the supply price of labor for these workers; the market clearing effect of flexible wages is not permitted to operate. In this context, high unemployment among groups of low-skilled workers—handicapped, youth, minorities—is inevitable, as is the persistence of income poverty among these same groups.

Two basic approaches are possible to correct these economic distortions, of which many were created by government policies, often in other areas and for other purposes. The first approach would be the direct elimination of the constraints—reducing the minimum wage and the disincentives of income-conditioned transfer programs and eliminating restrictive employer and union practices. The other is a second-best solution to ameliorate or offset the adverse side effects of these policies and practices, which occur in the form of wedges between employer-borne gross wages and the perceived marginal product of low-wage workers and between the net wage received by labor and the supply price of his or her work. It is precisely the reduction of these wedges which is accomplished by direct job creation programs. For employers, the program reduces the wage costs of hiring low-wage workers, while for low-wage workers, the program increases the possibility and reward of finding a job and holding it. In short, well-designed direct job creation programs can serve to offset the adverse side effects of labor market constraints and in so doing lead to increased employment and earnings of low-wage workers as well as increased output and aggregate employment with little or no inflationary pressure.

23

Guaranteeing "Equal Access" to a New Minority:
A Radical Rationale

There is a third type of justification for government intervention into the marketplace through disability policy.[13] The political response to this country's commitment to ending discrimination based on color was the historic civil rights legislation of the 1960s. Federal government intervention was justified as a means of guaranteeing equal justice, equal opportunity, and equal access to citizens regardless of color. During the 1970s that commitment led to major interventions into the private sector to redress discrimination. Affirmative action programs were the principal tool used to integrate racial minorities into white society. The revolutionary change in government policy toward the handicapped which occurred in the 1970s is based on a similar commitment by society to use these same techniques in order to integrate handicapped people into an able-bodied society. The implementation of that commitment— both then and now—is controversial.

Society's definition of disability rests on the fact that physical and mental attributes vary greatly among individuals. It is possible to rank these attributes (running speed, eye-hand coordination, and so on) with some degree of accuracy. Those below some measured level are considered by society to have functional limitations. Measuring the effect of these limitations with regard to a person's ability to function in society, however, depends on the existing network of relationships that links individuals to one another.

A work-disabled person is defined as one whose functional limitations are such that they lead to "job impairments." That is, they affect a person's ability to perform in a job. But clearly such a disability is a function of both an individual's condition and the structure of the job as it has developed in the economy. Functional limitations in themselves do not limit individual productivity. For instance, if the rules of basketball stipulated that the game was to be played by persons sitting in chairs with wheels, paraplegics would probably be highly productive players.

The revolution in public policy toward the handicapped in the 1970s was marked by the acceptance of the proposition that the handicapped represent a distinct minority group, in the same way that blacks and women are considered minority groups, which is subject to economic discrimination. That is, handicapped people possess characteristics that distinguish them from other members of society, and based on these characteristics they were "discriminated" against. Government's responsibility, then, was to reduce or eliminate this discrimination. The crucial implication of this justification for public intervention was that, just as one would not cure racial discrimination by making blacks white, the cure to the disability problem did not lie in reducing the functional limitations of the disabled. It did not lie in overcoming these limitations through traditional programs that shared the cost of disability through income maintenance, or in counteracting disability with increased training. Rather, it meant compelling society to change the network of private relationships which prevents this social minority from being fully integrated into all aspects of society.

This view recognizes that the handicapped are members of an oppressed minority whose ability to compete with able-bodied workers is impaired by the physical structure of the work environment and existing work practices—or whose entrance into the work force is prevented altogether because of these factors. The handicapped suffer this special discrimination in addition to the more traditional forms of stigma and prejudice jointly suffered with blacks and women.

Thus, rather than emphasize income maintenance or traditional work-related programs, some handicapped rights advocates argue that government guarantees of true access to a job is the best method of allowing handicapped people to enter the world of able-bodied individuals. The advocates of this rationale suggest, in addition, that even if all physical barriers to mobility were removed, the number of disabled adults who could find work and the job options open to those already employed would not necessarily increase substantially. Handicapped people's claim to a fair share of jobs and income will be satisfied only when the patterns of discrimination against disabled individuals in given plants, companies, or industries are exposed and government-enforced affirmative action plans are imposed.

In this section we attempted to place economic content around the concept of disability. The concept of the social cost imposed by disability became the key in viewing disability as an economic problem. This economic view of disability then provided the basis for considering the reasons government policies toward the disabled might, on economic grounds, be justified. We presented three types of economic justification:

a standard "neo-classical" justification based on welfare economics concepts, a "second-best" justification, and a justification based on civil rights. Each of these rationales underlies a particular form of government intervention; respectively, traditional income support and training or rehabilitation, direct job creation, and guarantees of "equal access." These three policy strategies are addressed in the remainder of the volume. We attempt to assess their economic impacts and, in the final chapter, to describe the nature of the debate that is likely to surround policy-making in all three areas in the 1980s.

3

Public Policy toward the Working-Age
Disabled: An Overview

Public policy toward disabled workers is reflected in a variety of programs, most of which are administered and funded by the federal government. Some of these programs have income support and some have rehabilitation as their basic objective; others seek to increase the demand for the labor services of disabled workers; and finally, and most recently, some are designed to assure equal access to employment, education, and mobility for disabled people. While this set of programs is targeted on disabled workers, it is in no sense a system. The programs are administered by several government agencies; the eligibility standards among the programs vary considerably; and while some encourage the disabled to work, others discourage them from working.

This chapter provides a brief overview of this set of programs. The objectives of each program, the definition of disability which it either implicitly or explicitly accepts, its size as indicated by number of beneficiaries and public expenditure costs, and additional program characteristics are described. To the extent that these programs are interrelated, the ways in which they interact are examined. Much of this discussion is summarized in the large table shown as Appendix A, which describes the four largest disability income support programs.

Income Support Programs

The major thrust of U.S. disability policy is income support. Most programs are designed to share the costs of handicaps widely among the

27

population. These programs are numerous, and their interrelationships are complex. They have grown rapidly, now accounting for about 17 percent of federal expenditures. The following discussion begins with the most general social insurance programs and moves to income support programs targeted on more particular groups of workers.

The Social Security
Disability Insurance Program

The Disability Insurance (DI) program is an integral part of the Old Age, Survivors, Disability and Hospital Insurance (OASDHI), commonly referred to as Social Security. The Social Security program is a compromise between an insurance program and an income redistribution program. In Social Security, unlike private insurance or annuity systems, a worker's potential benefits are only partially related to that worker's contributions into the system. The effect of this redistributive aspect of Social Security on saving and labor force behavior has been a major criticism of the system by those who oppose its dual insurance-income redistributive nature.[1]

The creation of DI as an addition to the Old Age and Survivors Insurance programs indicates that it, too, would try to satisfy both these goals. As a result, it is neither a perfect substitute for private disability insurance or a means-tested welfare system. To relate benefits to contributions a wage tax is used to collect revenue for the disability system, and benefits due are based on the worker's wage history. The first column of the table in Appendix A presents most of the economic characteristics of the DI program.

A few of the characteristics of this program are of particular note. First, the definition of disability in the program is a narrow one. It states that the worker must be impaired to the extent that he or she is unable to engage in substantial gainful activity (SGA) for a period lasting at least 12 months. Second, even though this criterion is a stringent one, there are a number of tests that are employed to determine eligibility, some which do give attention to the vocational characteristics of the applicant. Third, the operation of the program is divided between the federal and state governments. The federal government funds the program through a payroll tax and administers it through the Social Security Administration (SSA). While SSA established the guidelines for eligibility, the determination of eligibility is made by state government agencies. Fourth, the growth of the program has been rapid, in terms of both benefits paid and the number of benefit recipients. (This pattern of expenditure growth is summarized in table 3.1.) Fifth, the program rules severely limit the earnings of disabled workers. During a trial work period of twelve months, earnings above $280 per month ($300 in 1980) are allowed with no reduction in benefits. Upon completion of the trial work period, earnings in excess of the limit are considered proof of recovery and result in removal from the program. This is discussed further in chapter 5.

Finally, recipients of DI benefits also receive benefits from some of the other programs described in the remainder of this chapter. For example, about 10 percent of DI recipients also qualify for benefits in the welfare-based Supplemental Security Income (SSI) program. Similarly, all recipients of DI benefits for twenty-four consecutive months are also eligible for medical care benefits from the Medicare program. Indeed, in 1979, nearly $4 billion of Medicare benefits in the form of hospital care and physicians and related services went to DI recipients.

The Supplemental Security Income Program

Welfare programs aimed at the aged, blind, and disabled have been an important part of this country's income support policy since the 1930s. Like other of the nation's welfare programs, these have been operated by individual states, but under federal government regulations and with federal government financial support.

In 1974 the administration of these welfare programs was transferred from the states. A separate federal program—the Supplemental Security Income (SSI) program—was created, and a standard federal benefit schedule was established. States, however, are permitted to supplement these federal benefits. The second column of the table in Appendix A summarizes the principal characteristics of this program.

Eligibility for SSI benefits is based on a means test, which ascertains whether a person's income and assets are less than the specified national standards. As a means-tested welfare program, SSI has totally removed the link between contributions and benefits. It neither requires a given amount of previous work nor bases benefits on past earnings. In addition, its monies come from general revenues. The same definition of disability

Table 3.1 Annual Expenditures on Major Disability Programs, 1955–1980 (In Millions of Dollars)

Year	1955	1960	1965	1970	1972	1974	1975	1976	1977	1978	1979	1980
Disability Insurance (DI)	0	568	1,573	3,067	4,473	6,903	8,414	9,966	11,463	12,513	13,428	14,899
Supplemental Security Income												
State	0	0	0	0	0	45	70	76	81	84	95	100*
Federal†	135	236	417	976	1,393	2,557	3,072	3,346	3,628	3,882	4,286	4,912
Workers' Compensation												
Disabled and Dependents	521	755	1,074	1,674	2,009	2,745	3,205	3,735	4,495	5,223	6,104	
Survivors	70	105	140	197	235	315	360	420	482	531	600	
Hospital and Medical Care	325	435	600	1,050	1,250	1,760	2,030	2,380	2,680	2,958	3,356	
Black Lung												
Social Security Administration	0	0	0	110	554	951	948	963	942	965	983	1,032
DOL	0	0	0	0	0	0	9	17	25	58	729	808*
Veterans' Programs	1,982	2,530	3,026	3,930	4,498	5,141	5,583	6,147	6,709	7,000*	7,700*	8,100*
Railroad Disability Programs	155	204	190	275	325	434	451	505	529	570*	580*	650*
Government Employee Disability Programs	355	492	751	1,312	1,687	2,236	2,702	3,101	3,500	3,950*	4,500*	5,000*
Vocational Rehabilitation	42	96	211	704	876	968	1,036	1,190	1,260	1,296		
Rehabilitation Services (DI)	0	0	0	18	29	54	91	89	84	86	79	99
Medicaid	0	0	0	5,507	8,709	11,476	14,177	15,543	17,140	18,000*		
Medicare	0	0	0	7,149	8,819	11,348	14,781	17,777	21,543	25,204		
Total	3,564	5,421	7,982	25,969	34,857	46,937	56,927	65,253	74,603	82,030		

SOURCES: U.S. Department of Health, Education and Welfare, Social Security Administration (HEW, SSA) and U.S. Department of Labor, Employment Labor Standard (DOL, ELS). Additional data are from McMillan and Bixby (1980), p. 5.

*Estimated by authors from incomplete data.

† Prior to 1974 SSI data are payments to disabled persons under the Aid to Permanently Disabled and Totally Disabled Program.

used in the DI program is applied in the SSI program for the purpose of determining eligibility. The growth of program expenditures is shown in table 3.1.

The Workers' Compensation Program

The development of the Social Security Program paralleled a related development at the state level, in this case at the state government level. While the first workers' compensation program was enacted in the early 1900s and most states had pseudo programs by 1935, it was not until 1949 that all states had adopted workers' compensation programs. By 1978 over 90 percent of the labor force was covered by programs that would compensate for work-related injuries. These statutes presume that employers are liable for compensation at some level, but that they do not have to accept fault. By the mid-1970s all state programs also contained specific provisions for occupational diseases. The major force for maintaining a semblance of uniformity among these state programs has been the recommendations of periodic national commissions sponsored by the federal government.[2] The third column of the table in Appendix A summarizes the characteristics of this program and seeks to reflect the wide disparity among states in program structure.

While each state program is run differently, typically benefits are paid to covered workers who are temporarily disabled, whether partially or totally as well as to those whose impairments are permanent, whether partially or totally. The basis for determining the amount of compensation varies widely across the states. In some states, payments are determined by fixed tables that relate well-defined impairments (for example, the loss of the right hand) to compensation amounts. In others, compensation is determined as some fraction of estimated wage loss. The remaining states employ variants of both methods. In some cases compensation is made by periodic payments over time; for other cases lump-sum payments are made. Again, growth in program expenditures has been rapid, and is described in table 3.1.

The Federal Black Lung Program

In 1969 the federal government inaugurated a program providing benefits to coal workers with the symptoms of pneumoconiosis. Although it was invisioned as a relatively small program, by 1980 payments for benefits grew to nearly $2 billion. Table 3.1 summarizes the growth in federal benefit expenditures for this program from 1970 to 1980. The costs of the program and the demands for benefit programs by other groups with distinguishable illnesses have raised serious questions regarding the appropriateness of such categorical disease programs.

Prior to 1973 benefits were paid directly from the general fund of the Treasury. Funding claims since that time has become the responsibility of the Department of Labor, which shares compensation liability with coal-mining companies and their insurers. The federal share remains financed by the general fund. The program's basic benefit level in October 1980 was $280 per month for a single person, with additional benefits for spouses and dependent children. The maximum payment per family was $560. This benefit level is indexed to account for price increases.

Veterans' Disability Programs

Relatively unnoticed, but a large component among public programs aiding disabled persons, are the Veterans' Compensation and Pension programs. The Veterans' Compensation Program provides direct payments for service-connected impairments, and its benefit level is based on the estimated loss in earnings capacity attributable to the impairment. The sole eligibility requirement for the veterans' program is proof of an established service-connected impairment.

Benefits are paid in the form of cash, and they range from $38 per month for a 10 percent disability to $1,700 per month for loss of limbs or blindness. In 1977 about 2.3 million veterans received benefits. In addition, benefits are paid for over 600,000 dependents of veterans who have more than a 50 percent disability. A more detailed description of these characteristics is found in Appendix A.

The U.S. Veterans Administration also administers the Veterans' Pension Program, which provides assistance to veterans with war records who are permanently and totally disabled, irrespective of causes, if they have income and assets below specified levels. All *aged* veterans with war service are assumed to be totally and permanently disabled for the purpose of this program. Benefit rates vary widely, depending on other available income and the number of dependents.

In 1977, 3.3 million veterans received benefits from these two programs. Table 3.1 summarizes the level and growth of expenditures in both of the veterans' programs.[3]

32

Work-Related Programs

All of the programs described in the preceding section provide cash benefits to disabled workers; they are income support or wage replacement programs. There exists another large set of programs which provides services to the disabled, services often designed to increase the earnings capacity of the disabled and to facilitate their return to the work force. The program most directly targeted at disabled workers is the Vocational Rehabilitation Program. However, disabled people are also provided services designed to increase their work capacity from medical care programs. And, through direct job creation programs, including sheltered workshops, efforts are made to increase directly the demand for the labor services of disabled workers.

Vocational Rehabilitation

The Vocational Rehabilitation Program was initiated in the 1920s to ease the transition of World War I veterans into the labor force. Today, each state has a Vocational Rehabilitation Program that operates under federal regulations. The federal government pays up to 80 percent of the operating costs of these programs in addition to providing research, training, and capital grants.

The Vocational Rehabilitation programs focus on those physically or mentally handicapped persons who are judged to have the greatest chance of returning to work. Services of all forms can be provided the disabled person: medical and psychological care, training, and placement.

As table 3.1 indicates, the program has grown rapidly. Expenditures first exceeded $1 billion in 1975, when about 1.5 million people received services. Over 300,000 were claimed "rehabilitated," at a cost of about $3,000 per rehabilitation.

Medicare and Medicaid

Medicare and Medicaid are the two primary federal health-care support programs. The Medicare program provides payment for hospitalization and medical care costs of persons over age 65 and those persons who have received DI benefits for more than two years. In 1978 the costs of this program totalled $7.3 billion for physician and outpatient care and $17.9 billion for hospital and skilled nursing-home care; benefits were paid on behalf of approximately 15 million persons. The Medicaid program pays the medical care costs of public assistance recipients and other medically needy individuals. The program is a state-administered program that, in effect, procures medical services on behalf of the eligible population. States contribute between 17 and 50 percent of assistance costs as a supplement to the basic National Medicaid benefit. In 1978 total costs in the program were $18 billion, about $10 billion of which was borne by the federal government. Over 24 million people received benefits.

It is difficult to make the case that all of these expenditures provide assistance to disabled people. However, because most of the expenditures are for hospitalization, nursing-home care, or physician services, it is clear that the bulk of them are for individuals who at the time of receipt have some nontrivial impairment. A Rutgers University study suggests that 85 to 90 percent of such expenditures should be allocated to the disabled.[4] It should be noted, however, that many—and perhaps most—of the benefits are not paid on behalf of working-age disabled people. This is particularly true of the Medicare program, which is targeted on the aged. An alternative estimate, that of the Health Care Financing Administration, suggests that 50 percent of Medicaid and 12 percent of Medicare expenses are appropriately allocated to the disabled.[5]

Direct Job Creation Programs

Unlike a number of other countries, the United States does not have an organized employment program for disabled workers. However, public support in at least three forms is provided for the employment of handicapped workers. The first is a set of subsidy programs for which independent private or community sheltered workshops are eligible. The second is the direct creation of public service jobs for disadvantaged workers, defined to include the disabled. Finally, there is a relatively recent development, the provision of a subsidy to private employers for hiring handicapped (among other target groups) workers.

Sheltered Employment Sheltered employment[6] for the physically or mentally impaired takes place almost exclusively in special workshops designed to serve some subset of the disabled population. About three-quarters of these workshops are operated as private, nonprofit enterprises; the remainder are publicly owned, usually by local communities. For both types, government support—at both the state and the federal level—plays a major financial role, and increases in this support are largely responsible for the growth of the workshop system in recent years.

In 1950 about 400 shops were employing approximately 35,000 disabled people daily. By 1976, however, there were more than 3,000 shops and the daily employment of disabled workers had grown to about 155,000.

Government support flows through a variety of channels. Amendments to the Vocational Rehabilitation Act of 1921 provide federal assistance for rehabilitation facilities, including facilities located in sheltered workshops. Through these amendments and other recent legislation, subsidies are available for the construction of facilities, the hiring of a professional staff, and training, evaluation, and adjustment services. In the first two cases the workshop receives the subsidy, whereas in the third case the disabled worker is often the recipient. Subsidies are also available to help cover operating deficits. In 1973 the total subsidy to the workshop system was about $90 million. A reasonable guess for 1978 would be $250 million. In addition, workshops benefit from the Wagner-O'Day Act, under which goods provided by disabled persons are given priority in purchases made by the federal government.

Public Service Employment In the early 1970s government labor market policy began to focus on the structurally unemployed—specific groups that had high unemployment rates even when the economy was operating at full employment. Handicapped workers, youths, minorities, and those with little education were the main target groups. Reacting to the sustained high unemployment of these groups in spite of substantial and costly programs designed to provide education and training, the government began focusing on the demand side of the labor market. Funds were provided for the direct employment in the public sector of unemployed members of specified target groups, handicapped workers among them.

Most prominent among these public service employment policies is the Comprehensive Employment and Training Act (CETA). As originally developed in 1973, CETA was designed to enable local officials to coordinate manpower programs so as to meet their particular concerns and to provide jobs for unemployed and disadvantaged workers. Although the original act included a provision for public service employment for handicapped workers and others with low skills, the major thrust of CETA came with a 1974 revision that established an untargeted, counter-cyclical public employment program. With federal support provided to areas experiencing high and sustained unemployment, transition employment opportunities were provided by state and local government agencies at close to prevailing wage rates. Of the nearly 300,000 slots created in the first year of the program, less than one-half were filled by persons from low-income families, and nearly three-quarters were filled by high school graduates.

After 1976 the emphasis in CETA shifted toward disadvantaged, handicapped, and other hard-to-employ workers. The 1976 amendments reserved 250,000 job slots for disadvantaged and handicapped workers, and a target of 750,000 public service jobs was established, with eligibility criteria aimed toward disadvantaged and handicapped workers, welfare recipients, and the long-term unemployed. By 1979, 43 percent of the nearly 700,000 CETA jobs were being performed by the structurally unemployed, and by 1980 this figure had increased to about 55 percent.

Employment Subsidies   Direct job creation programs such as CETA involved the special provision of work by the public sector. Technically, workers in these programs were public employees. In the late 1970s, however, job creating efforts were also aimed toward the provision of jobs in the private sector, in part because the magnitude of the problem exceeded the potential of the public sector to provide jobs. The major private sector program designed to increase the demand for labor, particularly for low-wage labor, was the New Jobs Tax Credit (NJTC), enacted in 1977. The NJTC provided a tax credit equal to 50 percent of the first $6,000 of wages paid to workers hired in a firm above 102 percent of the firm's previous year employment level. While this two-year program (1977 and 1978) did not distinguish among workers by their unemployment, disability, or, poverty status, the subsidy was relatively greater for them than it was for more skilled workers, and as a result there was a greater incentive to hire low-wage workers.

In 1979 the NJTC was replaced by a directly targeted employment subsidy program, the Targeted Jobs Tax Credit (TJTC).[7] In this program private employers are provided a two-year subsidy of the wages paid for any member of a designated target group who is hired. The target group included youths from low-income families, disabled workers, Vietnam veterans, and SSI and general relief recipients. For the first year of employment this subsidy, paid as a tax credit, equals 50 percent of the first $6,000 of wage cost for any newly hired target group person. The subsidy falls to 25 percent for the second year of employment. By eliminating the 102 percent employment threshold and explicitly designating target groups, TJTC represents a shift in emphasis away from cyclical unemployment and toward structural, low-wage unemployment. The program has been in existence for such a short time that little data exists on the number of disabled workers being subsidized or their employment success.

Other Public Expenditure Programs Aiding the Disabled

The programs discussed in this chapter are the major public programs providing income assistance, services, or health care support to disabled persons. In 1978 expenditures on these programs totalled $82 billion (see table 3.1). Direct public expenditures made up 90 percent of this total. In 1977 the figure had been $74.6 billion.

In addition to those programs, there are numerous other programs of assistance or service provisions to the disabled. Appendix B presents a comprehensive list of these other programs, with actual or estimated 1977 expenditures shown. While most of these programs are designed for working-age disabled persons, some have target populations encompassing others, as well. In these cases, we allocate a reasonable percentage of expenditures to the disabled. On the basis of these percentages, the total expenditures in these programs are allocated between the disabled and nondisabled populations so as to provide a rough estimate of total annual public expenditures on disabled people. Expenditures on behalf of the disabled in these programs totals $23.3 billion.

Adding this amount to the $74.6 billion of expenditures on the disabled in the programs shown in table 3.1 produces a figure for aggregate public expenditures on behalf of the disabled in 1977 of $97.9 billion. If it is assumed that a reasonable estimate of the proportions of Medicaid and Medicare expenditures targeted on the working-age disabled are 50 percent and 12 percent respectively, this 1977 total falls to $70.4 billion.[8] It is this total that is used in the speculative calculations presented in what follows.[9]

In chapter 2 we concluded that there were about 21.3 million disabled working-age people in the United States in 1978, of which 10.8 million were severely disabled and another 4.7 million were occupationally disabled. If it is assumed that the $70 billion of public expenditures provided assistance only to the 21.3 million disabled people, the per person expenditure would be $3,286. If it is further assumed that each of these disabled individuals had one dependent, expenditures in support of the disabled and their dependents would total $1,643 per person. It is clear, however, that those disabled with but secondary work limitations do not receive substantial income support. If it is assumed that the total expenditures of $70 billion provided support to the 15.5 million severely and occupationally disabled, the per person expenditure would be $4,516. Again, assuming each such worker had one dependent would reduce this per person support figure to $2,258. Finally, on the assumption that the support is limited to the 10.8 million severely disabled individuals, the per person expenditures would be $6,481 with no dependents and $3,241 if each recipient had one dependent. Given the strict definition of disability employed in the DI program—one which excludes nearly one-half of all applicants—it would seem reasonable to estimate that the 1977 per person public expenditure on those disabled persons who were assisted was likely to have been in the $6,000 to $10,000 range.[10]

The large number of separate programs providing assistance to disabled workers is a serious impediment to evaluating the equity and efficiency impacts of the system. The potential for multiple program participation is enormous, making assessment of the distributional impacts of the system virtually impossible. With the long list of disparate programs targeted at disabled workers, it seems unlikely that an efficient and integrated pattern of assistance and service provision is attained. And the implications of this long list of programs for effective budgetary control are obvious. With an expenditure level of this magnitude at stake, the potential for reform is clear.

"Equal Access" Programs

In addition to financial assistance, rehabilitation, and direct job creation programs, there exists another set of public policies targeted at the handicapped. These policies are regulatory in nature and seek to impose standards on private business and public sector organization in their dealings with the handicapped. The objective of these policies is to provide handicapped people with equal access or equal opportunities in three aspects of their lives: employment, education, and mobility. The strategy here is to change the organization and functioning of the economy and society so that the attributes of the handicapped—such as lower earnings capacity and relative immobility—are ignored or compensated for in the economic and social arrangements by which society functions. Because these are rule-making policies, their costs are not reflected in public expenditures; nor are their benefits reflected in the numbers of people being supported or provided services. Rather, the costs of these policies are imposed on private or public sector organizations and become indirectly reflected in the prices of goods and services or in other public budgets.[11]

Athough this approach to disability policy has been discussed for many years, its implementation is a phenomenon of the 1970s. The primary legislation of this sort is the Rehabilitation Act of 1973 (PL93–112). Passed with vigorous support of organizations of the handicapped, using both the rhetoric and the tactics of the civil rights movement of the 1950s, this law (its title notwithstanding) seeks to force social and economic institutions to conform to the needs of the handicapped.

Section 501 of the act, for example, requires the federal government to develop and submit to the Civil Service Commission an acceptable "affirmative action program" for the hiring, placement, and promotion of handicapped individuals. This requirement is similar to that made of businesses and governments regarding the employment of blacks and women, and seeks to guarantee "equal opportunity."

Section 503 requires firms with government contracts in excess of $2,500 to take affirmative action in employing and advancing qualified handicapped individuals. Contractors with government sales in excess of $50,000 (or with fifty or more employees) must prepare and maintain an affirmative action program. But perhaps more important is section 504, which prohibits discrimination against qualified handicapped individuals in any program or activity receiving federal financial assistance, including programs providing employment, accessibility, education, health, welfare, and social services.

4

Economic Effects of Income Support Programs on the Working-Age Disabled

The Old-Age Survivors Disability and Hospital Insurance program (OASDHI)—commonly known as "Social Security"—is the largest single federal government program. Old-Age and Survivors Insurance (OASI) was instituted in 1935, and took its present form as part of the 1939 amendments to the Social Security Act. The major impact of these amendments was to change Social Security from a program based predominately on insurance principles—as it had first been envisaged—to one that attempted to achieve both insurance and income distribution goals. While a federal government commitment to the disabled population was part of this debate, the final form of these landmark amendments did not include any reference to the disabled.

The intense battle over initiating a disability system pitted two powerful groups with different philosophies against each other. There were those who believed that on both efficiency and equity grounds the disabled population should be protected by the Social Security system in much the same way that the system provided insurance and income distribution to the retired population. Then there were those who feared that the scope of any such program would inevitably expand far beyond that justified on efficiency grounds alone. Such expansion, it was feared, in addition to greatly increasing program costs, would induce a large reduction in the labor supply of fringe workers. And it was assumed that such a program would quickly become a general income support program, only partially related to the equity considerations associated with disability. Despite strong favorable recommendations by President Roosevelt and later by President Truman, these concerns over the ultimate fate of any federal disability system delayed the establishment of the disability insurance component of the Social Security program until 1954.

This chapter looks at the economic consequences of the current structure of federal income support policy toward the disabled working-age population. In evaluating the program, the cost effectiveness of its structure and operation are emphasized. That is, given that some level of federal intervention is desirable, the efficiency and equity consequences of that intervention need to be examined.

The specific issues addressed are: The determinants of the growth in disability program rolls and costs, and the role economic variables play among these determinants; the extent of work disincentives of public programs for the disabled and disabled workers' response to them; the relative impact of major disability programs on income replacement and the variation of this impact across income levels; and the primary shortcomings in the administration of programs for the disabled, and the extent to which these shortcomings are remediable.

The Growth of the Disability Insurance Program and Its Determinants

Changes in the Law

In 1954 disability was for the first time brought into consideration within Social Security, but only as a means of increasing future OASI benefits. A so-called "disability freeze" allowed workers judged to be disabled to collect OASI benefits based on their "healthy work history." But OASI benefits began at normal retirement age, not at the onset of the disability.

The foundation for the current Social Security Disability Insurance System (DI) was not laid until 1958, when disabled workers were first granted direct disability benefits. To be eligible for benefits a worker had to be aged 50 or over, had to have worked in twenty of the forty quarters preceding disablement, had to have worked in covered employment in six of the last thirteen quarters, and had to be judged unable to engage in

41

any substantial gainful activity (SGA) by reason of a medically determined physical or mental impairment that was expected to result in death or to be of continued and indefinite duration. Such a worker could begin collecting benefits after a waiting period of six months. These restrictions on the potentially eligible population have been increasingly liberalized over the history of the program. In 1958 dependents of disabled workers became eligible for benefits. In that same year the requirement of covered work in six of the last thirteen quarters was dropped. In 1960 the age restriction was dropped. In 1965 the duration of the impairment—inability to engage in SGA—was changed; it now meant that the disabling condition was expected to last at least twelve months or to result in death. And, in 1972, the waiting period was shortened from six to five months. These changes in the law are at least partially responsible for the growth in the program. (See Derthick [1979] for a fuller discussion.)

Changes in Interpretations of the Law

While the strict medical impairment criteria for eligibility in the DI program are emphasized, a vocational standard also exists. This standard considers such personal attributes as age, education, and work experience and is applied to workers whose impairments are not sufficiently severe to meet the strict medical standards. Although these vocational criteria have only been standardized in published form since 1978, they have played an important role throughout the life of the program.[1] Because these criteria are more subject to administrative discretion than the medical criteria, an expanded use of them in judging disablement is likely to have contributed to program growth. For example, in 1960, when the vocational criteria were still being formulated, less than 10 percent of all DI allowances were based on vocational factors. By 1975 these factors accounted for more than 26 percent of all allowances. While this evidence does not establish that the increase in allowances based on vocational factors has caused growth in the system, it is suggestive.

Also suggestive of changing interpretation of regulations and of the growing role of discretion is the increasing use of the appeals process. While determination of disability is initially made at the local level, the denied claimant has available at least four levels of review (a reconsideration, a hearing, an appeal, and the civil court). Koitz (1977) has suggested that there is a growing awareness of the advantage to be gained by pressing an appeal through this process. And there is evidence that appeals are being made more frequently. Initial applications for DI benefits have increased from 524,200 in 1965 to 1,279,100 in 1977. Reconsiderations have more than kept pace, increasing from 22 percent of cases denied at the initial level in 1965 to 28 percent in 1977. Hearings have increased even faster, from 20,100 to 140,700 or from 48 percent to 77 percent of cases denied at the reconsideration stage from 1965 to 1977. In 1965, 9.1 percent of initial DI recipients were first awarded benefits based on a reversal of their initial decision. By 1977 this had increased to 21.1 percent.[2] Such evidence suggests that increasing discretion in the interpretation of regulations has also contributed to growth in the DI program.

Changes in Benefit Adequacy

Individual DI benefits have significantly increased in both real and nominal terms since 1956. The increase is caused by the general increase in average lifetime wages (due to increases in both wage rates and the taxable maximum) on which the average monthly wage (AMW) calculation is based. But the increases are more directly due to ad hoc congressional increases in the Primary Insurance Amount (PIA) formula, on which DI benefits directly depend. Congress raised the PIA formula seven times between 1954 and 1974. After 1974 the PIA formula was automatically raised with increases in the consumer price index.

Table 4.1 shows that the potential disability benefits of the median manufacturing worker in 1957 with no dependents were $2,938 (in 1978 dollars). This rose to $5,265 in 1978. These data are stated in constant dollars, and thus this represents a real increase of 79 percent. Over this same period annual wages increased from $9,781 to $12,941 (in 1978 dollars). This is an increase of 32 percent. Hence, potential DI benefits for manufacturing workers have grown at more than twice the rate of real wages in the past twenty years. This is reflected in the replacement rate, which has risen from 30 percent to over 40 percent since 1957. Since DI benefits are exempt from income taxation, the increase in federal and state income taxes during this period for most workers makes the net increase in DI benefits even greater.

Changes in the law relating to the provision of benefits to a disabled worker's dependents have also increased the adequacy of the program. In

43

Table 4.1. Growth in Potential Disability Insurance Benefits and Wage Replacement Rates, Selected Years from 1957 to 1978

Year	Average Annual U.S. Wage, Manufacturing, 1978 dollars‡ (1)	Primary Insurance Amount, 1978 Dollars per Month§ (2)	Average Social Security Disability Benefit, With No Dependents, 1978 Dollars‖ (3)	Average Social Security Disability Benefit, Wife and One Child, 1978 Dollars# (4)	Wage Replacement Rate, No Dependents, Column (3) ÷ Column (1)** (5)	Wage Replacement Rate, With Wife and One Child, Column (4) ÷ Column (1)** (6)
1957	9,781	244.81	2938	5560*	30%	57%
1960	10,271	258.65	3104	6208	30%	60%
1965	11,556	270.42	3245	6490	28%	56%
1970	11,642	305.58	3667	6776*	31%	58%
1972	12,540	322.46	3871	7228*	31%	58%
1974	12,183	379.55	4555	8428*	37%	58%
1976	12,468	404.63	4856	8852*	39%	71%
1978†	12,941	438.86	5265	8779*	41%	68%

SOURCES: Consumer Price Index, 1957–1966: U.S. Department of Labor, Bureau of Labor Statistics (1975), p. 313. Consumer Price Index, 1967–1978: U.S. Department of Labor, Bureau of Labor Statistics (1979), p. 73. Average U.S. Weekly Wage, Manufacturing, 1946–1956: U.S. Department of Labor, Bureau of Labor Statistics (1970), p. 67. Average U.S. Weekly Wage, Manufacturing, 1957–1978: U.S. Department of Labor, Bureau of Labor Statistics (1979), p. 109. Method for Calculation of PIA: U.S. Department of Health, Education, and Welfare, Social Security Administration (1977), pp. 5–23); U.S. Department of Health, Education, and Welfare, Social Security Administration (1978c); and conversations with Social Security Administration representatives. Family Maximum Benefit Calculation: U.S. Department of Health, Education, and Welfare, Social Security Administration (1977), p. 24, and (1978b)), p. 5.

NOTE: All data are deflated using the Consumer Price Index, All Items (1967–100).

*Family maximum benefit applicable.

† Preliminary data.

‡ Calculated from average weekly earnings of nonsupervisory workers in manufacturing.

§ Primary Insurance Amount (PIA) for a 45-year-old male worker totally disabled in January of respective year with lifetime earnings history equal to the average wage earner in the manufacturing industry. The worker is also assumed to have no other Social Security covered income and to have been working since age 21.

‖ Annual PIA rate.

**Replacement rates in this table are different than those in tables 4.3 and 4.4 since this table reflects replacements specifically for the manufacturing industry; tables 4.3 and 4.4 reflect replacement rates for workers over all industries.

1958 DI dependent benefits were established. The full benefits paid to a disabled worker's family were set at a multiple of the worker's Primary Insurance Amount (PIA). A childless married couple receives no additional benefits, but each dependent of a worker with dependent children is eligible for an additional benefit of 50 percent of the worker's PIA.[3] A dependent spouse is eligible for an additional 50 percent of the worker's PIA if he/she is caring for a dependent child. Total family benefits may not, however, exceed the family maximum. The maximum for family members is limited to approximately 1.5 to 1.8 times the PIA of the disabled worker. Hence, total family benefits could range from 150 to 180 percent of the budgets awarded to a single disabled worker. Column 6 of table 4.1 shows that, for a disabled worker with a wife and one child, the replacement rate has risen from 57 percent in 1957 to 68 percent in 1978.

The availability of dependent benefits, together with changes in the law designed to increase relative benefits for low-wage workers, has made the program especially attractive for certain types of families. The families especially aided are large families headed by low-wage earners. As a result, some workers in this category are potentially eligible for DI benefits close to, or even in excess of, current wages. Lando and Hopkins (1977) found that in 1972 one-third of DI recipients had benefit levels in excess of 80 percent of their wage earnings in the year prior to the onset of disability, with one-quarter of newly entitled beneficiaries in 1973 receiving more in benefits than they earned in 1972. Moreover, as we have described, those receiving DI benefits for at least two years are automatically eligible for Medicare benefits. And a recent study by Van de Water (1978) predicts that 16 percent of newly awarded beneficiaries in 1979 will receive at least 80 percent of net earnings and that 6 percent will receive over 100 percent of net earnings.[4] A worker deciding between accepting DI benefits and continuing work will compare potential wage earnings and DI benefits. This evidence suggests that increasing benefit adequacy is likely to have contributed to the growth in the DI program.

Changes in the Costs of Benefit Applicancy

It takes time and effort for potentially eligibile workers to learn about the disability program, apply for benefits, and monitor their case through the Social Security system. These direct time and effort costs, however, are likely to be but a small proportion of the total costs of establishing eligibility. The worker must also endure the five-month waiting period. Moreover, except for trial work-period provisions, an eligible worker must abstain from engaging in any substantial gainful activity, meaning he or she cannot earn more than $300 per month. Meeting both of these constraints entails present and future reductions in labor supply. These reductions may be the most serious cost to potential applicants.

Clearly, a handicapped worker for whom any type of work is impossible will have no opportunity to earn wages. For such a person, the costs of gaining eligibility are only the time and effort costs. But the worker with a severe impairment who has the ability to continue working is in a quite different situation. This worker must consider whether the expected gain from DI benefits is sufficiently high to warrant refraining from substantial work over the five-month waiting period, in addition to confining earnings to below the SGA criteria ($300 per month) thereafter. It is this type of marginal case which appears to be increasing over the history of the system. As we have shown, vocational criteria are used in considering such a worker for benefits, and actual labor behavior will be important in the determination. The lost earnings in this case is a major cost of achieving beneficiary status.

It is because of the effect of such discretionary behavior that most investigations have included general economic indicators, such as the unemployment rate, in their analysis of DI growth. The notion is that the "sacrificed earnings costs" of gaining eligibility status will be smaller if the labor market is tight and job openings hard to find. Such models suggest that in addition to demographic, morbidity, and mortality changes over time, economic considerations may contribute to explaining the growth of both application and award levels over the history of the DI program.

Explaining the Growth of the DI Program

As table 4.1 illustrated, the real benefits of the DI system have grown considerably since the first benefits were awarded in 1957. The most significant growth occurred between 1969 and 1974; since then, the growth rate has slowed somewhat. In recent years a number of studies have been undertaken to estimate the contribution of the various economic, demographic, and institutional factors to the observed growth in the DI program. A description and critique of these estimates, focusing on the primary variables that have been considered, follows.

Unemployment Most empirical research has concentrated on the demand for DI benefits, looking at changes in the number of applications over the history of the system. These empirical analyses consistently find that both the absolute number of and the rate of applications increase with increases in the unemployment rate.[5]

A major cost of applying for DI is the waiting period and subsequent SGA limitations on work. This finding suggests that when a worker becomes unemployed, the cost of application (the waiting period and the limitations on work if eligible) is reduced, and supports the view that economic factors enter into the decision to apply for DI benefits.

This general finding leaves many questions unanswered, however. As Hambor (1975) points out, since the waiting period for eligibility was six months during the period of his study, one would expect a six-month lagged unemployment rate to affect applications significantly.[6] This was not the case. Similarly, while one would expect the application rate to be more sensitive to long-term (six months or more) unemployment or to the rate of workers dropping out of the labor force than to general unemployment rates, this result is often not observed.

Program Benefits As the value of DI benefits increases relative to market opportunities, an increase in applications would be expected. Rather than simply looking at real changes in the DI benefit, a number of studies have used a "replacement rate" variable in their analysis.[7] This variable was significant in the expected direction, again suggesting a behavioral response along economic lines.

Other Variables The growth in the eligible population has increased the number of applications. However, the application rate has also been increasing. A closer look at the changes in the age structure and the implications of the changes for the level of applications seems warranted. The incidence of morbidity increases with age, as does job separation and the probability of DI acceptance on vocational criteria. This indicates that as products of the baby boom of the 1940s reach age 50 and more, substantial increases in applications will occur.[8] In time series analysis, changes in the overall eligible population should be separated from changes in the age structure within that population.

It has been suggested that the proliferation of legal services for the poor that began in the 1960s has made it more likely that potential clients, especially if they are initially rejected, will be informed about the procedures necessary for DI application. Moreover, 1974 was the year in which the DI claims rate peaked and the SSI program was federalized.

Information about SSI and the consequent contact with the Social Security Administration (which administers SSI) could have led to an increase in applications. Studies focusing on this, however, have not found a statistically significant relationship between changes in public awareness and application rates.

Public attitudes toward the system often are suggested as being important to the application decision. A major argument in developing DI as a social insurance program outside of the welfare system is that such programs have less stigma attached to them than do social welfare programs. However, no empirical evidence exists on the degree of stigma related to DI or on changes in stigma over time, although it is thought to have decreased as the United States has come to transfer a greater share of its national income through the public sector.

Empirical data is even scarcer and less conclusive on the effect of changes in the supply of DI benefits than it is on the demand for them. There is little doubt that changes in DI regulations, together with the creation of disability benefits through SSI, have increased the number of potentially eligible people, but the impact of the administrators on awards is difficult to estimate.[9] Studies focusing on poverty levels and the ratio of actual awards to applications across states suggest the existence of nontrivial administrative discretion.[10]

Disability insurance has grown rapidly since it was first introduced into the Social Security system in 1954. The most important sources of that growth in the first decade of its existence were explicit changes in the law which, by 1965, had widened the eligible population by providing benefits at any age to both disabled workers and their dependents. Moreover, the time horizon in the definition of disability was liberalized from "an impairment that was expected to result in death or to be of continued and indefinite duration" to one "expected to last at least twelve months or result in death."

The decade after 1965 saw little change in the letter of the law, but there was an increased use of vocational criteria to establish disability, again increasing the eligible population. Over the first two decades of the program potential benefits increased at the same rate as wages, so that on average they replaced 30 percent of wages for a single worker and almost twice that for workers with dependents. While program growth increased during periods of high unemployment, economic factors were,

48

in our judgment, less responsible for program growth than changes in program rules which first expanded the eligible population and then lowered the eligibility standards.

Since 1972 increases in the generosity of program benefits also are likely to have contributed to program growth. Between 1972 and 1978 average replacement rates in the SSDI program increased 35 percent for workers without dependents and 17 percent for workers with dependents. And a large and growing group of the disabled were able to supplement DI benefits with those from other programs. The following section explores the effects of these disincentives.

The Labor Supply Effects
of Disability Programs

While the laws regarding eligibility for disability income support, and in particular for DI benefits, have been liberalized over the past two decades, they continue to be rigorous with respect to work.[11] An inability to perform substantial gainful activity remains the fundamental definition of eligibility in the dominant disability income support programs, the DI and SSI programs.

Nonetheless, given the incentives for reduced work effort created by these programs, there has been substantial concern about the labor supply effects of disability-related income transfer programs. These work disincentives stem from both the availability of benefits from the programs and the constraints that they impose on work effort if one becomes a recipient. Concern has risen with the increase in early retirement and the falling labor force participation rates of older workers. Our discussion focuses on this group of older workers and attempts to appraise the effect of disability transfers on the decision between continuing to work and seeking disability-related income support benefits.

The aggregate studies discussed in the beginning of this chapter suggest that application rates to disability income support programs are sensitive to overall economic conditions. Here the decision to apply for disability benefits is considered at the individual level. As we have previously noted, the working-age population with some type of self-reported impairment serious enough to restrict work was over four times the size of the DI beneficiary group in 1978. Even taking into consideration differences between self-reported and actual impairments, and the fact that some workers who are able to pass the medical eligibility tests are not covered by the Social Security system, it appears that a large segment of the population potentially eligible for disability benefits has not applied for them and does not receive them. Hence, the potential for labor supply reductions due to the benefit programs is still substantial.

Regarding those people whose impairments are severe enough to make market work nearly impossible or not possible at all, the system of disability income support policies will have no impact on labor supply. Informed of the program, this part of the impaired population will apply for benefits regardless of benefit levels or restrictions placed on work. Work restrictions are irrelevant for their decisions. However, for that group of impaired workers which could engage in market work, the disability policy system may substantially affect their decision whether to work or not to work.

These workers who are potentially eligible for disability benefits are faced with the choice between continuing in the labor market (working or searching for a job) and applying for benefits and adjusting labor supply behavior to conform to the eligibility rules of the program. For such workers, application does not guarantee acceptance. The risk of rejection may be high and the period of uncertainty long, even in the presence of an often-successful appeals process. The decision made by a person must weigh the expected value of uncertain benefits against the costs of application, which may involve reductions in the level of work and earnings to conform to the rules of the program.

Such a worker choice framework suggests several hypotheses with respect to the decision of a disabled person to continue working or to apply for disability income support benefits. For instance, the greater the potential loss in wages due to program-imposed constraints on the amount that can be earned if benefits are awarded, the smaller the probability of application. The greater the uncertainty in future wages and the less the uncertainty of program acceptance, the more likely application is. For those who have become impaired, the greater the negative impact of the impairment on potential (as opposed to historical) wage rates, the more likely application is. While benefits are related to historical wage rates, the decision to continue working after impairment depends upon the relationship between potential wages and the benefits available from other sources, including transfers. Hence, the more generous program benefits are relative to potential wages, the more likely application is.

Using some variant of this economic choice framework, researchers have attempted to test a number of these hypotheses. The primary hypothesis involves the effect of disability status and disability-related benefit levels on the choice between work or recipiency. Clearly, disentangling the effects of potential labor market earnings, potential disability-related benefits, and "true" disability on this choice is very difficult. Studies have experienced varying degrees of success in this effort. Here we briefly review and critique the major efforts to estimate the work effort impacts of disability policy.

One of the earliest of these studies was undertaken by Harold Luft, using 1967 data from the Survey of Economic Opportunity.[12] Luft was interested in the impact of disability on labor market activity: earnings, amount worked, wage rates. Using survey responses to questions regarding the extensiveness of functional limitations due to health, Luft separated the population into two groups, the disabled and the nondisabled. Then he estimated regression equations for the nondisabled group in which a variety of labor market indicators (labor force participation, hours worked, wage rate) are determined by a set of independent variables. These variables included age, education, family size, region, and so on. Having obtained coefficients for the nondisabled group, Luft used the equation to predict what the earnings of each member of the disabled group would have been if that person had no impairment. Luft finds that the health impact on labor market activity is substantial, and that it is much greater for blacks than for whites and for women than for men. He estimates that over 6 percent of total earned income is lost because of disability problems, and for individuals with limitations, the earnings decline ranges from 33 percent (white women) to 45 percent (black men) of expected annual earnings if limitations were not present.

These results are important in that they suggest that the presence of an impairment does lead to a major reduction in expected or potential income. These expected income losses make the work option less attractive for a disabled person, and conversely increase the relative attractiveness of being a recipient of disability transfers. However, the study has a number of weaknesses. The most important of these is the failure to control for the availability of disability income support benefits in estimating the loss of potential earnings. As a result, the earnings reduction that Luft attributes to disability should, in fact, be attributed to some combination of disability, access to disability transfers, and any other unmeasured

51

differences in the characteristics of the disabled relative to the nondisabled. The estimated earnings reduction attributable to disability is, therefore, exaggerated.

Two recent studies go well beyond these early results which, in effect, provided only circumstantial evidence that disability and disability-related transfers would induce reductions in work effort. The characteristics of these later studies—by Parsons and Leonard—are summarized in table 4.2. In the first of these efforts, Parsons explicitly adopts the sort of rational choice framework that we described earlier.[13] In his model, the individual rationally compares the expected values of being in and being out of the labor force. The value of being in the labor force depends on one's expected wage. The expected value of disability benefits and other transfers determines the value of not working. Because "true" health status determines the probability of receiving disability benefits, it too is a determinant of the labor force participation decision.

Using a unique index of "true" disability status—the mortality experience after one year of observation of the group to which an individual belongs—Parsons estimates a labor force participation equation for a sample of older men. The results he obtains are consistent with the rational choice framework. Expected disability and other income transfer benefits are negatively related to labor force participation and are statistically significant, as is the disability status variable. Moreover, the disincentive effects of expected transfer benefits increase with decreases in health status. Parsons finds the elasticity of labor force participation with respect to the generosity of disability-related transfers to be negative and significant but to vary substantially in the two variants of his study. Using earlier data, he finds that a 1 percent increase in the ratio of expected disability transfers to the wage rate increases the probability of labor force nonparticipation by 1.8 percent; using later data, the 1 percent increase in benefits results in a .6 percent increase in the probability of labor force nonparticipation. Both estimates, however, suggest a substantial negative work effort impact from the availability of disability-related transfers.

The issue in the Leonard disability transfer study[14] is the same as that in the Parsons study: Do increases in disability transfer benefits increase the probability of any given worker becoming a beneficiary (or equivalently, a labor force nonparticipant)? To address this question, Leonard fits a regression equation to data on 45- to 54-year-old males in which

Table 4.2. Labor Supply Analyses of Disability Insurance

	Study	
	Parsons (1980a, 1980b)	Leonard (1979)
Population analyzed	Men, 48–62(a) or 45–59(b)	Men, 45–54
Data used*	National Longitudinal Survey, 1969(a) or 1969(b)	1972 Social Security Survey of Health and Work Characteristics merged with benefit and earnings records
Dependent variable	Participation in work force	DI recipiency
Program variables	Potential DI/wage	Expected DI benefits
Specification	Probit	Logit
Results	Elasticity of non-participation with respect to re-placement rate- 1.8 (1966) or 0.63 (1969)	Elasticity of recipiency with respect to expected benefits - 0.35

*All are cross-section studies

the probability of disability beneficiary status is a function of expected benefits, expected labor income, and background characteristics representing taste differences.

Leonard finds that expected benefits are significantly and positively related to the probability of recipiency, and that the expected wage is significantly and negatively related to it. He finds that a $180 increase in annual disability benefits will increase the proportion of beneficiaries in the entire age cohort by one percentage point—equivalent to an elasticity of .35. Similarly, the higher the expected wage, the less likely one is to be a beneficiary. Applying these coefficients to time series data, Leonard finds that about one-half of the 4.5 percentage point decline in the labor force participation rate of this age group from 1957 to 1975 can be attributed to the availability of and increasing generosity of disability transfers.

The results of these studies suggest that decisions on "early retirement" and/or the receipt of disability transfers have a strong economic dimension to them. They also indicate that expected labor market earnings, expected disability transfers, and disability status all play a role in these decisions. Nevertheless, methodological and empirical weaknesses pervade these studies. While some of the later studies employ an appropriate maximizing choice framework, most do not. The disability status variables used to measure "true" health status are often very weak. They range from simple self-reported disability to future mortality and often give little indication of the severity of the impairment or its relationship to the demands of jobs for which the individual would otherwise be qualified. Further, expected disability transfers and nondisability transfers have been proxied by actual transfers, or other procedures that introduce misspecification have been used. Finally, little attention has been given to the role of labor demand conditions in explaining observed work effort status, and insufficient attention has been given to problems of simultaneity or selection bias in estimating the effect of changes in the availability or generosity of disability-related transfers to the work status choice. As a result, the precise size of the labor supply effect of disability related transfers has not been identified.

The decision made by current disability program beneficiaries to leave the program can be thought of in a similar maximizing framework. Consider a worker whose DI benefits are $400 per month (guarantee level) and whose impairment has improved enough so that he or she could earn $750 per month working full time. This worker is subject to the SGA test of $300 per month, and may earn this amount while keeping the $400 of benefits for a total income of $700 per month. However, at that point an additional dollar of earnings would lead to a loss of the $400 of DI benefits.[15] Because of this notch, a worker must be able to earn at least $700 per month to make up the loss in program income. Assuming a value of only $50 per month for the Medicare benefits that accompany DI, the worker would have to work a full forty-hour week, earning his or her capacity of $750 before the total income from working would equal the total income received by remaining on the program and constraining earnings to $300 per month.[16]

But even this example underestimates the potential impediments that a disability transfer recipient faces in leaving the program and returning to work. While DI benefits (as well as other income support federal benefits, such as SSI, Food Stamps, and Black Lung, for which this worker may be eligible) are not taxed, labor earnings are subject to federal, state, and local taxes. As a result, the gross earnings required to make program termination appear desirable would in this example approach $850 per month.

These studies and other pieces of evidence, then, do suggest that the availability and level of disability-related transfers—especially DI and

SSI—do induce workers with impairments to reduce work effort. Such reductions are required in order both to establish eligibility for the transfers and, if a person is receiving benefits, to maintain beneficiary status. While the level of this induced labor supply reduction has not been firmly established, its magnitude does not appear to be trivial. To some degree, then, the fears of the original critics of the system appear justified. Whether one considers the lost productivity from this labor supply reduction to be a major cost depends, of course, on how one views the cost-sharing responsibilities of society in response to the presence of disability.

Replacement Ratios and the
Adequacy of Disability Programs

Our discussion of the growth of and labor supply effects of the primary disability programs emphasized the influence of the economic characteristics of the program on the application and labor supply decisions of workers. A key element in that discussion was the possible incentives such programs have on work effort. While this is a major concern of policy-makers, it must be tempered by the knowledge that disincentives are an inevitable side effect of any program that attempts to provide assistance to the handicapped population.

This section focuses on what is considered by many to be the primary goal of disability programs: to provide an adequate offset to earning losses and especially, adequate protection against poverty for those who become disabled. This is what we described earlier as the cost-sharing function of government policy and reflects both the "collective compassion" and the equity basis of collective action. From the discussion in the previous section, however, it is clear that the work effort effects of replacement rates do not lie far below the surface of the present discussion. We estimate the adequacy of the three major public programs, measuring the extent to which their potential benefits would replace lost earnings as well as the extent to which they protect workers against falling below the poverty line.

Replacement Rates

Ideally, one would define the relationship between potential program benefits and potential wage earnings as the program replacement ratio.

Because of the difficulty of identifying these potential values, we employ a proxy. In table 4.3 we assume a disability level and compare program benefits with a preimpairment wage. Thus our replacement rate is the fraction of after-tax, preimpairment wages which is replaced by program benefits.[17] In the table, estimates are shown for three prototypical workers, each in a family of two persons, who experience impairments indicating total permanent disability. They differ only in their wage-earning histories. The first earns one-half the annual wages of the median worker over his or her lifetime, the second exactly the median, and the third earns twice the median. Wage replacement rates are shown for all three in 1968 and 1978. We further assume that each worker is eligible for benefits in only one of these programs at a time.

The table indicates a major increase in replacement rates over the past decade in all of the programs. For the largest program, the Disability Insurance program, the net replacement rate for the average income worker rose from 35 percent to 49 percent between 1968 and 1978. For the average income worker, replacement rates in the Workers' Compensation and SSI programs changed relatively little. The variance in benefit levels among the states is still substantial in both of these programs, however; for example, for the average income worker in 1978, the replacement rates in the SSI program vary from about 25 percent in the low benefit states to about 42 percent in the high benefit states. The tables also indicate that all of the programs are equalizing, providing a higher replacement rate for the low-wage worker than for the worker with twice the annual income. As would be expected, the SSI program, as a welfare program, has a higher replacement rate for low relative to high wage-workers than the other programs.

Although the replacement rates calculated do not yield precise estimates of the potential wages replaced by disability benefits, they do provide *lower* bounds on potential wage replacement. Given the estimates in the tables, then, it is reasonable to speculate that potential wage replacement is at least 60 percent for most workers at or below the average income level. The expected effect of this wage replacement on labor supply is difficult to disregard. Given the certainty of benefit recipiency relative to the uncertainty of market work, the choice in favor of beneficiary status is even stronger. The implications for labor supply of the marked increase in replacement rates over the past decade is also noteworthy.

56

Income Adequacy

Since the 1960s a major benchmark for measuring the effectiveness of public policy has been the degree to which social programs have removed people from poverty. The poverty line is defined as the minimum level of income necessary to provide an adequate living for a family of some given size.[18] It has been argued that, at a minimum, public disability programs should provide a "safety net" for the working population which would keep them from falling into poverty if they became disabled. Table 4.4 provides evidence on the extent to which such a safety net exists. Again, the situations of three prototypical workers, each in a family, who experience impairments indicating total permanent disability are analyzed. The workers differ only in their wage-earning histories. The first worker earns one-half the average annual wage of the median worker over his or her lifetime, the second exactly the median, and the third earns twice the median. Here we assume a four-member family consisting of a disabled worker, a spouse and two dependent children. The degree to which potential benefits from each program match a poverty income level is found for both 1968 and 1978. We further assume that each worker is eligible for benefits in only one of these programs at a time.

A major finding of table 4.4 is that, while it was still possible in 1978 for workers to fall into poverty because of total disability, it was far less likely than it was in 1968. The major variation appears to be across the states rather than across programs. In states such as Texas, which provides no state supplement to SSI, for instance, only 34 percent of poverty-line income is guaranteed, while in California the guarantee is 59 percent. With respect to DI, the median worker is guaranteed benefits above the poverty line. It is those who, even when they are healthy, have near poverty-level earnings who are most likely to fall below the poverty line if they become totally disabled. But it is exactly this type of worker that is most likely to be eligible for both DI and SSI. In addition, there are still other programs not presented here which are likely sources of income support to such a worker, primarily Food Stamps and Medicare. When benefits from these programs are cumulated, it is likely that few workers eligible for disability benefits, DI or WC, will fall into poverty.[19]

These calculations show that for the great majority of workers who become sufficiently disabled to be eligible for DI, SSI, or Workers' Compensation, benefits are large enough for them to remain above the poverty

Table 4.3. Potential Disability Benefits and Income Replacement Rates for Three Hypothetical Workers in Two-Member Families under Major Disability Programs, 1968 and 1978

	Benefit Provided and Income Replacement Rate					
	Worker Earning One-Half Average Annual Income during Lifetime of Employment		Worker Earning Average Annual Income during Lifetime of Employment		Worker Earning Twice Average Annual Income during Lifetime of Employment	
Disability Program	*Disabled in 1968*	*Disabled in 1978*	*Disabled in 1968*	*Disabled in 1978*	*Disabled in 1968*	*Disabled in 1978*
Disability Insurance						
Annual benefit rate	$1,102	$2,904	$1,606	$4,470	$1,876	$5,937
Gross income replacement	43%	59%	31%	45%	18%	30%
Net income replacement	45%	59%	35%	49%	21%	35%
Disability Welfare						
California						
Annual benefit rate	$1,866	$3,864	$1,866	$3,864	$1,866	$3,864
Gross income replacement	72%	78%	36%	39%	18%	20%
Net income replacement	77%	78%	41%	42%	21%	23%
Texas						
Annual benefit rate	$1,164	$2,273	$1,164	$2,273	$1,164	$2,273
Gross income replacement	45%	46%	23%	23%	11%	11%
Net income replacement	48%	46%	25%	25%	13%	13%
Workers' Compensation						
District of Columbia						
Annual benefit rate	$1,617	$4,586	$3,235	$6,115	$3,640	$12,229
Gross income replacement	63%	93%	63%	62%	35%	62%
Net income replacement	67%	62%	45%	43%	24%	23%
Oklahoma						
Annual benefit rate	$1,617	$3,051	$2,080	$3,900	$2,080	$3,900
Gross income replacement	63%	62%	40%	39%	20%	20%
Net income replacement	67%	62%	45%	43%	24%	23%

Worker's expected annual income, 1968			
Before tax	$2,574	$5,147	$10,294
After tax	$2,439	$4,589	$ 8,789
Worker's expected annual income, 1978			
Before tax	$4,943	$9,887	$19,774
After tax	$4,943	$9,147	$16,925

NOTES: At time of disability, each worker is assumed to be age 45, male, head of a two-person family with a nonworking wife, totally disabled as of January 1968 (or January 1978), receiving no outside income in any form, and taking the standard deduction on federal income taxes. All replacement rates assume the worker is covered *only* under the program in consideration. No adjustment for state tax liability is included.

U.S. average annual income here is for workers with taxable earnings under OASDHI, that is, covered employment, plus contributing self-employment persons. Farm and nonfarm workers are included. The income measure used here is *not* the same as used in table 4.1; hence the replacement rates presented here may vary from those in table 4.1 for comparable years.

Table 4.4. Potential Disability Benefits Relative to the Poverty Level for Three Hypothetical Workers in Four-Member Families under Major Disability Programs, 1968 and 1978

| | Benefits Provided and Benefit as a Percentage of Poverty Level | | | | | |
| | Worker Earning One-Half Average Annual Income during Lifetime of Employment | | Worker Earning Average Annual Income during Lifetime of Employment | | Worker Earning Twice Average Annual Income during Lifetime of Employment | |
Expected Income and Poverty Level:	Disabled in 1968	Disabled in 1978	Disabled in 1968	Disabled in 1978	Disabled in 1968	Disabled in 1978
Worker's expected annual gross income in year of disability:	$2,574	$4,943	$5,147	$9,887	$10,294	$19,774
Poverty level in year of disability:	3,531	6,630	3,531	6,630	3,531	6,630
Disability program:						
Disability Insurance						
Annual benefit rate	$1,558*	$4,033*	$3,117*	$7,764*	$3,960*	$9,095*
Percent of poverty level	44%	61%	88%	117%	112%	137%
Disability Welfare						
California						
Annual benefit rate	$1,866	$3,864	$1,866	$3,864	$1,866	$3,864
Percent of poverty level	53%	58%	53%	58%	53%	58%
Texas						
Annual benefit rate	$1,164	$2,273	$1,164	$2,273	$1,164	$2,273
Percent of poverty level	33%	34%	33%	33%	33%	34%

Workers' Compensation

District of Columbia						
Annual benefit rate	$1,617	$4,586	$3,235	$6,115	$3,640	$12,229
Percent of poverty level	46%	69%	92%	92%	103%	184%
Oklahoma						
Annual benefit rate	$1,617	$3,051	$2,080	$3,900	$2,080	$3,900
Percent of poverty level	46%	46%	59%	59%	59%	59%

NOTES: The hypothetical workers have the same characteristics as those in table 4.3 except that they are household heads of a four-member family. A spouse and two dependent children make the family eligible for additional benefits subject to a family maximum. The poverty level is that reported by the U.S. Bureau of Census for a four-member family. The figures used here are weighted averages of farm and nonfarm workers' poverty level incomes.
*Maximum family benefit rate.

line. However, as we discuss more fully in chapter 5, for those with impairments or poor health not sufficient to make them eligible under DI, no strong "safety net" exists. Much of the current debate with respect to the "welfare" role that the DI program should play centers around the provision of aid to this majority of the impaired population.

Issues of
Program Integration and Administration

As documented in chapter 3, the public commitment to handicapped people has resulted in a myriad of programs, each of which affects in some way this population. The problems associated with such a diverse network of programs can be considered at two levels. The first potential set of problems result from basic conflicts resulting from incompatible program goals. These fundamental conflicts, which are discussed more fully elsewhere (see especially chapter 6), include the relationships between the insurance and welfare goals of disability income programs; between program adequacy and the creation of work disincentives; between work- and income-related restrictions and program benefit; and between work- and income-related restrictions and rehabilitation and job creation efforts.

A second potential set of problems are more program specific and follow directly from the possibility of multiple program eligibility and administration. Handicapped people may be eligible for several programs simultaneously, depending on the nature of their disability, its source, and their current work and income status. As studies by Johnson, Cullinan, and Curington (1978), Conley and Noble (1973), and Muller (1980) show, there is significant overlap between the principal sources of benefits for impaired workers: Social Security Disability Insurance, Workers' Compensation, veterans' benefits, and private insurance. A study by Conley (1975) provides some evidence on the degree of program overlap for those currently receiving Workers' Compensation. It shows that a significant number of recipients of permanent total Workers' Compensation benefits also receive benefits from other programs. Of those receiving permanent Workers' Compensation benefits, over 50 percent also receive DI benefits, and 13 percent receive private benefits.

Using the 1972 Social Security Survey of Health and Work Characteristics matched with the Master Beneficiary Record of the Social

Security Administration, Muller (1980) has estimated the extent of multiple beneficiaries among those receiving Disability Insurance. He found that 43.9 percent of the Disability Insurance population had multiple benefits in 1971. Within this group 87 percent received benefits from only one other source and 12 percent from two other sources. Veterans' benefits was by far the largest overlapping program; 21 percent of total recipients studied received veterans' benefits. Private employer pensions were the second largest; 9 percent of the recipients received additional income from this source. Disability welfare (APTD/AB) was third, with approximately a 6 percent overlap. Only 3 percent of the Disability Insurance recipients also received Workers' Compensation. Muller (1980) also found that the total benefits received by multiple beneficiaries was, on average, twice that of those receiving only Disability Insurance. In addition, the median income replacement rates for multiple beneficiaries was 1.5 times that for those receiving Disability Insurance.

Another set of integration problems concerns the multiagency involvement in the administration of benefits and/or services. For example, while the federal government, through the Social Security Administration, pays for DI benefits, state employees handle the determination of eligibility. As stated earlier, the Vocational Rehabilitation Program is administered by the states, with block grants made with DI funds providing additional financial support. SSI is financed by federal income taxes, but states are given the option of providing additional support. As in DI, eligibility for SSI disability benefits is determined at the state level.

While the variation in state supplements is the prerogative of the states, serious questions have been raised as to whether state determination of DI awards should be continued. At the federal level, the Social Security Administration has the authority to reverse state agency allowances of disability, as well as to move forward the determination of the onset of disability. It does not have the authority to reverse state agency denials. Prior to 1972 SSA reviewed the vast bulk of state agency decisions on a "preadjudication" basis (that is, before the decision was made and the claimant informed). The allowances and denials which it questioned were returned to the states. The administrative cost of this level of review (as well as the backlog caused by the introduction of the Black Lung Program) led to its replacement by a 5 percent sample review in 1972. In 1974 the review became "post adjudicative."

Critics assert that these changes were "penny-wise, pound-foolish," in that the resulting loss in quality assurance outweighs the saving in administrative costs. A recent (1976) General Accounting Office (GAO) study found that DI determinations lack uniformity. A sample of 221 cases selected from actual claims settled in one state were sent to other state agencies for determination. There was complete agreement among the states on only 32 percent of the cases. GAO recommended more uniform training, better guidance on policy changes, and better documentation of evidence at the district office (Koitz, 1977).[20] Yet it is difficult to argue that it is the federal-state system that is responsible for this nonuniformity in determination. As we have seen, in addition to a medical criterion, a vocational criterion is used in determining awards. It may be that the inevitable subjectivity inherent in these criteria is responsible for much of the variation. The number of reversals in the review process also suggests that variations in determination procedure exist throughout the program.[21]

Another potential problem related to state administration of federal programs like DI and SSI is that states have a vested interest in easing standards. To the degree that potential welfare recipients (who must be paid at least to some degree directly from state revenues) can be put on federal programs, the state support burden can be shifted to the federal government. The importance of this incentive is not known, although there is some evidence that the state of New York has attempted to take advantage of this method for reducing its welfare responsibility (Sunshine 1979).

As public policy has developed with regard to the disabled population, the administrative conflicts that are the inevitable results of our multi-program approach to this population have increased. Individuals covered by work-related disability programs such as Workers' Compensation or veterans' benefits comprise a subset of those who are also eligible for Disability Insurance, which protects workers who become disabled regardless of where or how the disability occurs. Private disability insurance is available to cover disability developed on or off the job and interacts with government provided insurance. Programs like Black Lung, which are disease specific, or SSI, which offers protection to the disabled regardless of work history, are two different types of programs aimed at specific portions of the disabled population. These programs interact with the others. The justification for a multiprogram approach to disability is that it is able to protect those who would "fall through the cracks" of a system with less overlap. While this may be a benefit, the redundancy costs of such a system also are clear.

The fear that any federal program for the disabled would expand beyond that justified on efficiency grounds alone has been borne out by the first twenty-five years of disability policy in the United States. The system has quickly expanded from a narrow, medically defined disability system to one that includes job-related as well as health-related criteria. In addition, the emergence of SSI has provided welfare benefits to some part of the disabled population regardless of work history.

Given the moral commitment to the "deserving poor" which has long been a part of our nation's history, this result is neither surprising nor necessarily disturbing. Clearly, public policy over the first twenty-five years of the system has responded to both efficiency and equity arguments in accepting an increasing share of the full costs caused by the onset of disability.

The system now provides a strong safety net that virtually guarantees that no worker who is severely disabled will fall into poverty. Further, it guarantees that those who are severely disabled from birth will be assured a minimum income. The budget costs of such protection have not been small; for the present, however, they have leveled off. However, a price has been paid in terms of lost productivity. This is caused by the reduction in work effort of fringe workers who are induced to quit work in order to receive disability benefits. Such inducements are part of the reason for the drop in labor-force-participation rates of middle-aged and older male workers over the last two decades.

Many features of the overall disability policy are possibly not cost effective and could be changed with little loss in protection from poverty. Given the emergence of SSI as an effective income distribution tool, some of the redistributive features of DI are now redundant. In addition, the multiprogram aspect of the system causes unnecessary administrative complications, while it does little to protect people from "falling through the cracks." It appears the costs of providing multiple coverage are difficult to justify when compared to the benefits derived.

5

Economic Effects of Work-Related Programs for the Disabled

The discussion to this point has centered on the provision of income support to the disabled of working age. But public policy has traditionally provided training, counseling, and job-placement services designed to return the disabled to active participation in the labor market. As we discussed in chapter 4, these supply-side rehabilitation and training approaches to integrating the disabled into the work force have a long history. Rehabilitation and training programs have been joined by sheltered workshops in this integration effort. This type of government involvement on the demand side of the job market represents the only significant government job-creation program geared toward the handicapped prior to the 1970s.

The first part of this chapter discusses the economic consequences of these two traditional approaches to integrating the handicapped into the work force. The benefit-cost evaluations that have been made of both rehabilitation and sheltered workshop programs are reviewed and critiqued, and then their efficiency potential is discussed. A look at the new job creation programs follows. These programs, developed during the late 1970s, were designed to increase directly the availability of work for the disadvantaged. In each of these programs, handicapped workers were included in the target population. Four economic problem areas concerning these programs are discussed: displacement, budget, valuation of output, and administrative and design. Again, the perspective of benefit-cost analysis is used in the discussion. Finally, some comments on the likely economic impacts of "equal access" regulations are offered. Because this strategy has been introduced and implemented so recently, the discussion can only be impressionistic.

Traditional Work-Related Programs

As we have noted, rehabilitation and training efforts, often in a sheltered workshop context, have long been an integral part of government policy toward disabled workers. As a result, evaluation of and research on these programs are far more fully developed than they are on the newer types of work-related programs, direct job creation and equal access policies.

The Effectiveness of Rehabilitation Programs

Vocational rehabilitation services are provided on the state level, but 80 percent of the cost is financed through grants from the federal government. In 1978 federal government expenditures on vocational rehabilitation totaled $1.3 billion.

A work-oriented strategy such as vocational rehabilitation is a substitute for public income support and reflects a quite different philosophy regarding the provision of public services to disabled workers. Income support programs are cost-sharing efforts; rehabilitation and training programs can be viewed as investments designed to reduce the social costs of disability. The two approaches, however, interact with each other, sometimes complementing each other but often working at cross purposes. For example, generous public income support is likely to reduce the incentive to work, hence reducing the probability that training or rehabilitation policies will be effective.

Ultimate evaluation of relative merits of the two approaches depends on the efficiency and equity impacts of both policies on the disabled working-age population. The primary concern with an income support strategy is the incentive it provides for labor supply reduction and public expenditure growth. This was discussed in chapter 4. With respect to rehabilitation policies, then, the question is: Do these policies yield employment and earnings benefits in excess of their costs, or do they fail to meet such an efficiency test?

Table 5.1. Taxonomy of Benefit-Cost Components for Rehabilitation Programs

Financial Analysis

Benefits	*Costs*
Increased taxes due to earnings increases	Program expenditures
Reduced income support payment due to earnings increases	

Efficiency Analysis

Benefits	*Costs*
Present value of earnings increases due to rehabilitation	Labor costs of the rehabilitation activity
Sociopsychological benefits of rehabilitated worker	Capital costs of the rehabilitation activity
	Foregone income of the client during rehabilitation
	Foregone productivity from displacement of other workers due to employment of the client

Analyses of the effectiveness of rehabilitation programs have been of two types. The first type concerns studies undertaken to determine whether government expenditures on rehabilitation yield government budget savings in excess of the expenditures. These in essence are financial studies focusing on the impact on net public revenues of publicly financed rehabilitation. The second type of study involves standard benefit-cost analysis techniques to evaluate the full social efficiency impacts of rehabilitation programs. The difference between the two approaches is shown in table 5.1. In the financial analysis account, all of the benefits and costs accrue to the government budget; the entries in the economic analysis account refer to the social efficiency gains and losses of the program. The focus of the following is on the benefit-cost studies that attempt to estimate the social efficiency of the programs.[1]

Beginning in the early 1960s, numerous studies of the economic effects of vocational rehabilitation programs were undertaken. Almost uniformly, these studies yielded estimates of benefits relative to costs which were very high—benefits of twenty times the costs were not unusual.[2] The procedures in these studies were standard: the earnings of program clients after they received training were compared with their earnings in the period (week, month, year) before training, this difference was projected into the future (sometimes with adjustments for normal productivity growth or expected job loss), and the discounted present value of this gain was compared to the discounted present value of program costs (sometimes with adjustments for foregone income during training and other components of cost not directly stated in program accounts). These studies employed crude benefit-cost techniques: no control groups, suspect before-after earnings comparisons, guesses regarding the permanence of initial earnings increases into the future, and failure to consider some components of real costs. As a result, they were generally viewed with suspicion, though the sizable benefit-cost ratios produced did not lead to serious doubts regarding the overall economic worth of the program.

Perhaps the most well known of these benefit-cost studies was that by Conley in 1965, which he followed up with additional data in 1969. Conley uses the difference between earnings during the year prior to the acceptance of a person into the program and earnings after the case is closed by the agency as the earnings increment attributable to the program. After projecting this difference into the future, discounting it to the present, and comparing it to the real cost of the program, Conley concludes that vocational rehabilitation is a worthwhile social investment. At a discount rate of 8 percent, the benefit-cost ratio ranges between 3.5 and 4.5 over the several years of the analysis.[3] Conley also analyzes the program from the perspective of the government budget (the taxpayer perspective) and finds that the reduced benefits paid plus increased taxes received cover the program costs in from 3.5 to 5 years. Finally, he finds some evidence that the program may produce larger net benefits for treating the less, rather than the more, productive among the disabled.

Conley's procedures and assumptions have been challenged widely. In particular, the absence of a control group, the failure to use a multivariate model, and the assumptions made about the persistence of the earnings increase have been cited. Subsequent studies have attempted to improve on Conley's work, in terms of both benefit-cost methods and data.

This next generation of work was more sensitive to the need to control for factors other than the training program—for example, race, sex, age, and degree of disability characteristics of recipients—which could also affect earnings. Both Bellante (1972) and Worrall (1978) improved upon Conley's methods. The results, however, were similar. But again, no control group was employed, the external effects of the program (such as the psychic well-being of the client and his family) were not measured, and it was assumed that no displacement of nonrehabilitants by rehabilitants occurred.

One of the results yielded by these studies concerned the impact of the program on specific groups of program clients: age groups, racial groups, sex groups, and types of disability. Conley, for example, suggested on the basis of his results that the benefits of providing services to low productivity groups—older workers, those with little education, blacks, and those with severe disabilities—might be more efficient than those achieved by supplying them to groups who have been more successful in the labor market. Bellante and Worrall, however, found that it is more efficient to provide services to the young, the married, and less severely disabled people. This general conclusion was also reached in a study by Berkowitz and Rubin (1977) using 1970 data. These studies only calculate the average benefit-cost ratios of rehabilitation services supplied to various groups of disabled workers. However, decisions on program allocation among various groups require information of the effects of expenditures on the margin—that is, marginal benefit-cost ratios.

What can be concluded from these studies? First, in terms of a social benefit-cost criterion, the vocational rehabilitation program does appear to yield substantial net benefits. Although the available studies are methodologically flawed, it seems unlikely that improved procedures and data would overturn the results. However, because the benefit-cost calculations yield average rather than marginal benefit-cost estimates, little evidence exists on the efficiency of expanding the program beyond its present size. Second, although the evidence is not strong, it appears that concentrating rehabilitation activities on younger, less disabled, and more productive workers is likely to be more efficient than focusing on the less productive of the disabled group.[4]

In determining the effectiveness of rehabilitation efforts, it must be remembered that disability is defined with respect to the performance of the economy. If a handicapped person's functional limitation does restrict his or her ability to compete in the labor market, society has several options. On the one hand, it may seek to rehabilitate the person so that the impediment can be overcome. Alternatively, society may seek to adjust prevailing economic conditions so that the impairment becomes less relevant. Or, society may choose to compensate the handicapped person directly through an income support, cost-sharing strategy. Finally, a strategy incorporating aspects of all these approaches may be chosen. Benefit-cost analysis of rehabilitation programs, holding constant the income support system and the performance of the economy, is likely to yield different results from those obtained by an analysis in which these other aspects of the system are also allowed to vary.

This last point deserves emphasis. For lower productivity workers, as most of the disabled are, the notion of a labor market queue is appropriate in considering the potential impacts of rehabilitation programs. In such a queue, less severely disabled workers stand ahead of those with more severe handicaps. In a fully employed, high-demand economy, both workers at the front and those far back in the labor queue are likely to find employment. Rehabilitation and training in such a regime is likely to enhance the earnings of all workers in the queue. However, with low demand, workers back in the queue are unlikely to be employed. The implications for rehabilitation programs in this low-demand situation are important. Training provided to the most severely disabled is less likely to generate employment and earnings gains in such an environment than it is in a high-demand situation, and is less likely to improve earnings and employment of these workers than it is those with less severe disabilities. In a low-demand, high-unemployment situation, then, the advisability of concentrating resources on rehabilitation services rather than job-creation strategies (such as sheltered workshops or employment subsidies) seems open to question, as does the strategy of focusing training resources on more rather than less severely disabled persons.

The implications of low-labor demand for rehabilitation and the focus of such services on the most severely disabled are reinforced by another effect. Less severely disabled workers are far less likely to be eligible for disability-related income support than are those with more severe impairments. Indeed, in both the DI and SSI programs, support is available only to those presumed to be unable to work. As a result, the earnings available in the labor market have to be substantial for these workers if the labor market option is to dominate transfer recipiency status. For severely disabled workers, then, the availability of income transfers impedes the rehabilitation and training effort. For all of these reasons, concentrating limited rehabilitation resources on the most severely disabled seems questionable.[5]

The Effectiveness of Sheltered Workshops

As we have noted, most sheltered workshops[6] are run by private, nonprofit agencies. However, since the passage of the Vocational Rehabilitation Act of 1921, increasing federal assistance for rehabilitation facilities located within these workshops has been provided. Although these expenditures are only a small part of overall federal disability expenditures and only 20 percent of federal expenditures for vocational rehabilitation, they grew substantially in the 1970s, from $90 million in 1973 to over $250 million by 1978.

Regular sheltered workshops reflect their rehabilitation genesis and have as their goal the provision of transitional employment designed to enable the worker to pass successfully into the able-bodied work force. Skill training is not emphasized. This mission was supplemented in the 1970s by a separate program for the severely disabled, who were judged to have low productivity in the job market. A series of "work activity centers" was established to provide longer term or even permanent employment to these handicapped workers. An evaluation of the ability of sheltered workshops to meet stated goals in an efficient manner is in order. While the equity or redistributive aspects of the program may be significant, they are not considered within the context of benefit-cost analysis. A comprehensive taxonomy of benefits and costs with which the efficiency performance of sheltered workshops may be evaluated is presented in table 5.2.[7]

Two major studies of sheltered workshops have been done in the United States. The first, by Greenleigh Associates (1976), looked at 400 workshops in 1974. The conclusions were quite optimistic, showing that sheltered workshops yielded $1.56 worth of social benefits for every dollar of social cost, when benefits were discounted at a 10 percent rate. The benefit-cost framework used in this study, however, is seriously deficient. On the benefit side, the Greenleigh Associates study only considered the value of the increased productivity of program participants resulting from sheltered workshops. On the cost side, they included only expenditures made by the workshop. Thus only financial, and not resource or opportunity costs were included.

A more sophisticated study of sheltered workshops was done by Christiansen (1981). This study merged the Greenleigh data with that from the U.S. Department of Labor. His overall results are more pessimistic than those of the Greenleigh Associates study. In addition, the variations in the value of per-client workshop output are instructive, since they show the diversity among sheltered workshops as well as the great divergence in productivity of various handicapped people. By far the most

Table 5.2. Taxonomy of Benefit-Cost Components for Sheltered Workshops

Benefits*	Costs†
1. Value of program output	1. Foregone client output
2. Present value of increased productivity of clients	2. Program operating costs, including supervisory salary costs, machinery & facilities costs, and incremental training costs
3. Sociopsychological well-being increase to client	
4. Reduced medical or psychological care costs stemming from increased client sociopsychological well-being	3. Value of foregone output from displacement of private sector and normal public sector resources not re-employed
5. Third-party benefits stemming from increased client sociopsychological well-being	

*Social benefits from one year's operation of the program.
† Social costs from one year's operation of the program.

productive handicapped were the blind, who averaged over $8,500 in direct benefits.[8] This is compared to $3,500 for those classified as generally handicapped and $1,000 for the mentally retarded. The superior performance of the blind clients is due to both their higher level of skill and the greater amount of productive capital equipment in their workshops. Those in regular program workshops had nearly seven times the output per person as those in work activity centers. This is not surprising, however, since work activity centers were established to create jobs for the most severely disabled.

Christiansen's empirical results compare the per client value of partial net benefits under optimistic and pessimistic assumptions for different types of clients and shops. The value of output produced plus the increased productivity of the clients less all of the costs defined in table 5.2 yields an estimate of "partial net benefits." Under optimistic assumptions the net social loss is $1,112 per client; under pessimistic assumptions this rises to a loss of $2,152 per client. When estimated third-party benefits are included, however, a much more optimistic result is found. These benefits, in chapter 2 referred to as aspects of "collective compassion," reflect the attitudes of the able-bodied public to improvements in the economic status of the handicapped. When these effects are included with the optimistic assumptions, a net social gain is registered; with the pessimistic assumption net losses of about $1,800 per workshop client are recorded, even with the third-party benefits.

73

Among the handicapped, third-party benefits attributed to the blind rank very high, and exceed the contributions to the mentally retarded under either set of assumptions. These social benefits increase what was a modest net benefit for regular program workshops into one of about $2,300 per client under optimistic assumptions, as well as turning a loss into a small gain for work activity centers.

These results suggest that channelling resources toward severely disabled clients—for example, via work activity centers—yields substantially smaller economic welfare gains than when efforts are targeted on the moderately disabled. The output of severely disabled clients will certainly be low, and, as mentioned previously, resources devoted to rehabilitation and training do not appear significantly to enhance the productivity of this group. This is not to say, however, that tilting federal programs toward the most severely disabled for income distributional purposes is not justified. These distributional gains must serve to offset the probable net efficiency costs of the programs.

There is a great range of physical and mental impairments among handicapped people of working age. The Rehabilitation Act of 1974 announced a change in the allocation of public expenditures for rehabilitation purposes toward the most severely disabled workers. It is difficult to make definite judgments on the potential success of this effort based on the limited evidence available. However, it is clear that the cost of creating jobs for the most severely disabled is high and the value of the output from such jobs low. Hence, unless a high value continues to be placed on the sociopsychological aspects of these jobs, their efficiency as a mechanism for meeting the "collective compassion" aspects of disability policy appears open to question. The verdict on regular sheltered workshops, however, is much less pessimistic. If only moderate weight is given to characteristics of the job itself, these shops appeared to yield net social gains. However, the available evidence is based on average benefit-cost calculations rather than marginal ones, and is based on data from the early 1970s.

Direct Job Creation
for Disadvantaged Workers

The federal government has made a modest effort to use traditional work-related programs to integrate handicapped workers into the work force. The issues in this area concern the efficiency of these programs and on whom they should be targeted. Running parallel to these specifically designed job-creation programs for the handicapped was a major change in government policy toward direct demand-side government intervention in the job market for all disadvantaged groups: racial minorities, those with little education, women, as well as handicapped. By fiscal year 1980 nearly $4 billion was obligated for direct job-creation efforts for the disadvantaged, and three-quarters of it went to public sector job creation.

Support for direct public job provision came from many quarters. It included those who wanted to substitute "work" for "welfare" on both the right and the left. But it also came in part from a belief that selected additional government interference in the market could reduce constraints on labor market performance of disadvantaged workers. By counteracting these constraints (that is, minimum wage and welfare policies, discriminatory employer behavior, the power of trade unions), direct job creation promised to be an effective instrument for reducing income poverty, and for solving what has come to be known as the structural unemployment problem.

As discussed in chapter 3, the most prominent among the recent policies fitting this definition is the Comprehensive Employment and Training Act (CETA). As originally developed in 1973, CETA was designed to enable local officials to coordinate manpower programs so as to meet their particular concerns and to provide jobs for unemployed and disadvantaged workers. In fact, this did not occur. Despite the specification of the handicapped as a disadvantaged group, few job slots were filled by handicapped or other disadvantaged workers. Of the nearly 300,000 slots created in the first year of the program, fewer than one-half were filled by persons from low-income families, while nearly three-quarters were filled by high school graduates. Like employers at rehabilitation and sheltered workshops in the 1960s, CETA employers, for various reasons, were not anxious to hire workers with severe work productivity problems. This included those they perceived to have physical and mental handicaps, as well as those with poor work habits.

After 1976 the emphasis in CETA shifted toward disadvantaged and hard-to-employ workers. The 1976 amendments reserved 250,000 job slots for disadvantaged workers. And, with Carter administration sponsorship, a target of 750,000 public service jobs was established with eligibility criteria targeted toward handicapped and other disadvantaged workers, welfare recipients, and the long-term unemployed. By 1979, 43 percent of the nearly 700,000 CETA jobs were being performed by the structurally unemployed; by 1980 this increased to 57 percent. While this significantly affected the poor, only a small number of jobs went to the handicapped, and few went to those with severe disabilities.

Direct public jobs provided by CETA or its predecessors (Operation Mainstream, Neighbor Youth Corps, or work incentive programs) were funded publicly. Technically, workers in these programs were public employees. In part due to the fear that political patronage was a more important criterion than being disadvantaged, and in part because of economic efficiency reasons, by the mid 1970s direct job-creation efforts were increasingly aimed toward the provision of jobs in the private sector.

The major private sector program designed to increase the demand for labor, particularly for low-wage labor, was the New Jobs Tax Credit (NJTC), enacted in 1977. As was discussed in chapter 3, the NJTC provided a tax credit equal to 50 percent of the first $6,000 of wages paid to workers hired in a firm above 102 percent of the firm's previous year employment level. While this two-year program (1977 and 1978) did not distinguish among workers by their unemployment, disability, or poverty status, the subsidy was relatively greater for them than it was for more skilled workers, and as a result there was a greater incentive to hire low-wage workers.

In 1979 the NJTC was replaced by a directly targeted employment subsidy program, the Targeted Jobs Tax Credit (TJTC). A private employer is given a tax credit equal to 50 percent of the first $6,000 of wage cost for the first year of employment of any newly hired person from a designated set of categories: youths from low-income families, disabled workers, Vietnam veterans, and SSI and general relief recipients. The subsidy falls to 25 percent for the second year of employment. By eliminating the 102 percent employment threshold and explicitly designating target groups, TJTC represents a shift in emphasis away from cyclical unemployment and toward structural, low-wage unemployment.

With the change in administrations in 1981, prospects for continued emphasis on these demand-side, direct job-creation strategies faded. Along with the general skepticism toward public spending came the judgment that the costs of this particular form of labor market intervention exceeded the benefits forthcoming from it. Four basic criticisms of these direct job-creation efforts targeted on disadvantaged workers in general and the handicapped in particular emerged in the debate.

The first problem associated with direct job-creation programs involves "displacement effects"—the reduction of employment somewhere as an offset of the job-creation impacts of the program. Because the primary objective for this strategy is employment creation, its evaluation must be in terms of its net job-creation impact, defined as the difference between the employment level in the economy with the policy and that without it. Clearly, because (1) the output produced by the subsidized workers competes with alternative outputs, (2) the financing of the program entails opportunity costs that represent displaced outputs, and (3) some of the subsidized workers would have been working in the absence of the subsidy, the *net* job creation impact will be smaller than the *gross* number of workers hired or subsidized. The ratio of net to gross job creation is an indicator of these displacement effects.

Although several studies have estimated this ratio or its equivalent for public employment programs, estimates vary widely. For example, one evaluation of CETA, in which few constraints were imposed on the governmental units that administered the program, suggested that this net-to-gross jobs ratio approached zero in the long run. The implication is that fiscal authorities were able to divert nearly all of the CETA funds to expenditures that would have been financed alternatively in the absence of CETA. In general, the short-run net employment effects were found to be larger than the long-run effects (see Johnson and Tomola, 1977). Other studies evaluating public employment programs—and critiquing the above study—were more optimistic. They placed the ratio of net-to-gross employment at between 40 to 60 percent after one year—implying that about one-half of the funds were diverted from job creation through "fiscal substitution" (Borus and Hamermesh, 1978).

So far there have been no reliable evaluations undertaken of the more recent Targeted Jobs Tax Credit (TJTC) programs. There have been evaluations of the New Jobs Tax Credit (NJTC) program, however. Because of the crucial differences in the targeting provisions of these two programs, however, findings on the latter can only be suggestive as regards the former. In the NJTC evaluations, studies measured the net gain in employment of displacement within industries, but failed to consider the possible displacements in other sectors of the economy. In one study, the employment increases in the construction and retailing industries attributable to the NJTC were estimated by means of a variety of time series regressions (Bishop and Haveman, 1979). The estimated NJTC employment stimulus over the twelve-month period from mid-1977 to mid-1978 ranged from 150,000 to 660,000. For these industries, total employment growth over the period was 1.3 million. The preferred models attribute at least 20 to 30 percent of the observed employment increase in these industries to NJTC. Other studies, based on different data and techniques, also suggest a substantial effect of the NJTC (Perloff and Wachter, 1979).

A second problem involves the resource and budget costs of the net jobs created by this approach. The budget costs per *net* job created appear to be quite high. The most recent "guesstimate" of budget cost is based on the assumption that displacement is 20 percent in public employment programs and 80 percent in private sector job-creation programs. It suggests a cost per job for private sector programs of about $6,500, and a cost for public sector programs of over $9,000 per job. Although these estimates do not consider the increased tax revenues generated by the extra employment or the reduced transfer payments, they do suggest that the taxpayer cost per job created is close to, if not in excess of, the net earnings of the new employees.

This discussion of budget costs per job raises a third problem—the valuation of the output produced relative to the real costs of creating the jobs. As discussed in the section on sheltered workshops, the benefits attributable to such jobs involve not only the productivity of the worker while he or she is employed on the job, but also the contribution of the work experience or on-the-job training to his or her earnings in the future. The real costs of employing a worker in such a special public or private program include both the value of the equipment and materials with which he or she works, the value of supervisory and associated administrative personnel, and the value of what the person would have been doing if the program had not existed. This foregone productivity might involve the worker's alternative market activities, or the home production (for example, child care) in which he or she would have been engaging, or simply the value of the foregone leisure.

This economic efficiency criterion is a difficult one to meet for either private or public sector direct job-creation efforts targeted on severely disabled or other low-productivity workers. Diverting such workers into a direct job-creation program is likely to entail relatively small losses from alternative activities (especially if the alternative to participation is involuntary unemployment), but these workers do require associated inputs in the form of materials, equipment, and supervisory personnel, all of which comes at full cost. The key issue, then, is the value of the output produced. Because the output of public job-creation programs is not marketed, its value is hard to measure. This is especially true if the basic motivation for the program is the provision of psychological or sociological benefits, work experience, or training to members of the target groups, rather than the achievement of some defined objective or the production of some identifiable good or service. The evidence on the direct benefits of sheltered workshops suggests that such programs may well not be cost effective unless a significant value is placed on socio-psychological benefits. This is especially true for programs targeted on the severely disabled.

The final problem concerns the administrative and design problems associated with direct job-creation programs. Such programs are exceedingly difficult to design and administer, and they are surely more costly than income support programs. The administrative difficulties of public service employment have already been referred to. The problems associated with employment subsidy programs are equally difficult but of a quite different sort. For example, a marginal wage subsidy such as the NJTC will minimize displacement (and windfalls to employers), but will be relatively ineffective in targeting the additional jobs created. On the other hand, a program that is effectively targeted on severely disabled or disadvantaged workers may find recruitment costs high, employment goals unattainable, and output objectives difficult to achieve.

The realities of direct job creation in the 1970s served to temper the optimistic economic rationale for its use as a strategy for the 1980s. The early 1970s enthusiasm for jobs programs designed to reduce unemployment and poverty was generally dampened by the realities of implementation.

The new administration has rejected direct public job creation as a means of increasing the job potential of disadvantaged groups. Hence 1980 will likely be viewed as the high-water mark for CETA. But the administration's position on targeted job subsidies as part of a strategy to offset impediments to work is not as clear. One approach to these impediments is to eliminate them—for example, regulations constraining labor mobility or wage rate adjustment, such as the Davis-Bacon Act or the minimum-wage law, could be repealed. An alternative strategy would be to implement a targeted job subsidy program which would offset the constraining effects of labor market regulations on minimum-wage laws. This second alternative would be less offensive to labor unions and others who see a general reduction in minimum-wage laws or the repeal of regulations as a threat.

Yet another alternative to both job subsidies and the repeal of regulations would be to provide an *employee*-based employment subsidy arrangement. Until now, both of the major private sector job-creation efforts (the NJTC and the TJTC) have been employer-based. The employer verifies whether newly hired workers qualify under the terms of the legislation for a subsidy, and if they do, a claim for payment is filed. The workers need not know if they generate the subsidy, nor will coworkers know. Moreover, in such an *employer*-based plan, individual workers have little ability to influence the hiring process, even if they know they are in the target population. Response to the incentive lies only with the employer, and, as a result, any activities induced by the subsidy to match job to worker will be only on the demand side of the market. The labor supplier is a passive participant.

This incentive pattern would be altered if the subsidy were employee based. For example, assume that each worker certified as a member of the target group were given a card indicating that any employer hiring the worker would be entitled to a subsidy of a designated form. Indeed, the subsidy terms could be identical to those in any employer-based targeted program. Possession of the card would provide the worker with a labor market advantage, and hence an incentive to search for a job. Knowing the rules of the program, the employer would have no less incentive to match job to worker than he or she had with an employer-based scheme. The advantage of such an employee-based plan, then, stems from the increased incentives to the labor suppliers to search for work, which increases the probability that they will be hired.

In evaluating such an arrangement, several questions immediately arise: (1) Would workers feel stigmatized if they were specially certified as card- or voucher-holders? (2) Would coworker resentment be generated if noncertified workers sensed special conditions or if retention probabilities were associated with holding a certification card? (3) Would employers confront added (or reduced) administrative burdens if employee certification were handled in this way? (4) Are there possibilities for varying the terms of the subsidy depending on the circumstances (such as income level, age, or region) of the worker? (5) Would target-group members already employed be eligible for a certification card, and would their employers be eligible for the subsidy? (6) If the subsidy were paid only for hiring a new certified worker, would not artificially induced job turnover be created? Given the benefits from the increased job-seeking activities which an employee-based plan would induce, the answers to these questions would have to be rather strongly negative to warrant abandonment of this idea without further consideration.

"Equal Access" Regulations

Chapter 3 described the "equal access" policy developments in the 1970s which are best represented by the regulations implicit in the Rehabilitation Act of 1973. This policy required both private and public employers to hire disabled workers and enforced this requirement through the courts. The model for this approach was the affirmative action procedures that grew out of civil rights activities.

This approach is a radical one, and goes well beyond the traditional income support or rehabilitation strategies, or even the more recent direct job-creation legislation. The objective of the "equal access" strategy is to alter directly the productive process of society. Until now, the impact of these laws on daily activity in United States society has not been great. The lawsuits brought have been few, and the settlements have not been particularly onerous.

The potential of this legislation for imposing major cost increases on private business and other governments is substantial. Unfortunately, no reliable estimates of the extent of these costs have been made. However, when one contemplates the changes required by these regulations if they were to be fully enforced, the total bill is not likely to be substantially less than that entailed by environmental and occupational health and safety (OSHA) regulations. Moreover, the implications of these regulations for productivity change and economic growth do not seem to differ greatly from those of environmental and OSHA regulations.

Uncertainty about the cost impact of the Rehabilitation Act of 1973 was no doubt partially responsible for the long delay in the issuing of

Department of Health, Education, and Welfare regulations implementing the act. Amid nationwide sit-ins by handicapped groups, the regulations were signed in April of 1977 and became effective on June 3, 1977.

These regulations are far reaching. They argue that "equal opportunity" means more than simply allowing handicapped people the right to enter public facilities. The regulations stipulate that the termination of discriminating treatment is not sufficient to ensure equal opportunity, additional positive action must be taken—the individual handicap must be considered. A recent court decision, for instance, required a college to provide a hearing-impaired student with her own translator so that she could attend classes. What is yet to be determined with respect to the new laws is the degree to which society must provide "equal opportunity." Cost or difficulties have been ruled to be appropriate considerations in fashioning remedies when a recipient of federal funds has been found to be discriminating. What remains to be determined is the extent to which such costs will be weighed against the benefits in the interpretation of the regulations.

The introduction of such cost considerations into decisions relating to the enforcement of equal access regulations is quite contrary to the intent of the advocates of this policy approach. To them, equal access is a fundamental principle, and its achievement is to be secured as a matter of right, irrespective of cost. An alternative point of view, however, is that the "equal access" goal differs little from other important objectives in the disability area, such as efficiently sharing the cost of impairments or undertaking efficient investments to reduce the cost of disability. In this perspective, the costs of securing more equal access must be set off against the benefits that a reduction in inequality conveys. And no absolute level of access inequality is to be set as inviolable.

It is this alternative, benefit-cost, perspective that has guided our discussion of the economic effects of the traditional income support-rehabilitation-training policies, and that of the newer direct job-creation efforts as well. And in our view it is this perspective that should guide any ultimate evaluation of the equal-access strategy. If one accepts the principle that less inequality in access is desirable, even if full equality in access is not feasible, the issue becomes little different from those confronted earlier. How much should inequality in access be reduced, and toward what dimensions of inequality should major efforts be directed? With this framework, benefit and cost comparisons must be made and difficult choices confronted. Ultimately, evaluation of the effects of the equal-access efforts will depend on the relationship of the benefits that are achieved relative to the costs required.

Perhaps the best way to illustrate the difficult choices required in moving toward "equal access" is by an example. Consider briefly the federal regulations to assure an equal-access urban mass transit system surrounding the so-called Transbus controversy. Because the federal government subsidizes nearly all the local government bus purchases, it has the ability to set standards for new buses to be produced and sold. Under section 504 of the Rehabilitation Act of 1973, Congress required the Department of Transportation (DOT) to set standards for buses to make them fully accessible to the handicapped. "Transbus" represents the set of specifications which any new bus must contain to meet the requirement of "full accessibility." DOT has mandated that transit authorities must purchase only Transbuses after September, 1979. Unfortunately, no bus manufacturer, domestic or foreign, has been willing to produce buses that conform to this design.

A newly designed bus that provided significantly greater access to the handicapped than any previously operated bus has been built and is available for purchase at two-thirds the projected costs of Transbus. This improved bus, however, has not been purchased in the quantities expected because of its nonconformance with Transbus specifications and uncertainty over its future compliance with DOT regulations. This appears to be a case of the "best" being the enemy of the "good." The desire to improve access to the handicapped has delayed the improvement of existing facilities, at least in the short run.

A useful way to determine whether such delays are justified is to envision varying degrees of inequality in access to public transportation. The present situation contains major impediments to facility use by the handicapped—inequality is substantial. Transbus, on the other hand, forces the development of new technology substantially to equalize access. An intermediate option would involve making currently available modifications to existing buses to provide access to the great majority of handicapped people. Specially-designed minibuses could supplement these buses and serve the severely handicapped (especially the wheelchair-bound). Each of these options has a set of benefits and costs associated with it, and as one moves to increasingly small levels of inequality, greatly increasing costs are likely to be incurred. Either formally or in-

83

formally, society must find a way of comparing these costs and their associated benefits.

For those who make a strict legal interpretation of equal access, the intermediate case does not appear to be acceptable—in civil rights language, it is viewed as "separate and therefore unequal." To take this position, however, and to refuse to consider another transportation option, one must argue that the benefits of the Transbus increment exceed the additional costs of Transbus. Consider first the utilization benefits of the Transbus option. Getting on a bus is only one of the burdens handicapped people face in using a bus system. The architectural environment together with weather conditions restrict the handicapped from getting to buses and waiting for them. The availability of fully accessible buses would only slightly increase the utilization of them by the handicapped. It is not at all clear that the utilization of Transbus will be as great as that of the intermediate door-to-door paratransit system.

The full costs of Transbus are far from certain. It is apparent, however, that "full accessibility," when it is defined as access to all means of transportation, requires a major commitment of resources. Transbus is only part of this commitment. The costs of converting fixed rail facilities are equally expensive. Some estimate the total cost of full accessibility to ground transportation at $8 billion. It is essential that some process determining the relative costs and gains from increased "accessibility" be established. Only then can the use of scarce resources to achieve only small increments in benefits to the handicapped be avoided. Only through such a process can the real welfare gains from improved access be kept separate from the achievement of an arbitrary standard or principle.

A first step in this process was taken in a recent report by the Congressional Budget Office (1979), which argued that implementing the equal access to transportation provisions of section 504 would be expensive— the report estimated $6.8 billion over the next thirty years—and would benefit relatively few handicapped persons. Three alternative options for providing transportation services to handicapped persons living in urban areas are evaluated in the report. The conclusion drawn is that providing a mixture of currently available "kneeling buses" and dial-a-ride vans or a mixture of kneeling buses, vans, low-fare taxi service, and a provision of special equipment for automobiles is significantly less expensive than the current DOT "equal access" plan. It is estimated that the DOT plan would serve no more than 7 percent of all severely disabled persons, at approximately $38 per trip, whereas the two mixed plans discussed above would serve 26 and 30 percent of all severely disabled, at $7.62 and $7.33 per trip, respectively.

In addition to the transportation area, the "equal access" issue pervades a wide range of other areas as well: the design of public buildings, sidewalks, entrances to commercial establishments, curbs—indeed, the architectural design of entire communities. In all of these areas, steps toward reduced inequality of access can be taken. And while benefit-cost considerations are often ruled out, as they were in consideration of civil rights issues, some mechanism for establishing priorities in the face of limited taxpayer willingness to pay must be achieved.

As indicated, it is still too early to put forth even a tentative evaluation of the economic effects of the equal access regulations. It can be suggested, however, that without a cost-conscious implementation of these regulations, ultimate evaluation of this strategy is likely to find that the costs imposed on society are in excess of any potential benefits experienced by the disabled.

6
Issues in the Disability Policy Debate

Since World War II, government policy toward the disabled of working age has concentrated on programs designed to share directly the costs of disability by providing income support to the most severely disabled. These programs, together with the provision of moderate amounts of assistance for rehabilitation, sheltered work, and direct job creation, formed the core of the disability policy system until the 1970s. In the mid-1970s direct job creation and the provision of equal access to employment, education, and mobility emerged as major additions to the arsenal. As we look at the prospects for the next decade, it seems clear that a critical turning point has been reached. The conflict over the objectives, structure, and adequacy of the current income support programs directed toward the working-age handicapped is likely to continue, as will the reevaluation of these programs brought on by the change of administration in 1980. But the differences in philosophy concerning these programs is minor compared to the differences concerning programs that involve government more directly in the marketplace. The intervention of the federal government on the demand side of the labor market through creation of jobs for the handicapped people—a policy initiative of the late 1970s—is likely to be a highly controversial aspect of government policy in the 1980s. Even more controversial is the new sense of self developed by the handicapped community in the 1970s which caused a radical reconsideration of their rights in society, and which is now being challenged. The major commitment by the federal government to assure "equal access" to employment, education, and mobility in order to integrate fully handicapped people into the broader community resulted in a major increase in government intervention in the private sector. This intervention forms part of the tangle of regulations criticized by the new administration as costly and ineffective.

This chapter discusses the continuing struggle over the proper role of government policy toward the working-age disabled by dividing current policy issues into three broad areas of likely conflict. It also discusses some of the policy choices that must be made in these areas during the 1980s.

The first area of conflict is likely to focus on the role the disability system plays in general income support strategy, or, more generally, in income redistribution policy. That is, what is the appropriate level of disability cost which should be borne by society at large, and by what criteria should assistance to the disabled be allocated among potential claimants for it? In formulating this role, choices must be made which affect the system's eligibility criteria, the breadth of protection it provides, and its tax and benefit structure.

The second area, while not independent of the first, concerns the role a disability system plays in aggregate employment policy. Policy choices made in this regard determine the responsibility of the program to contribute to a reduction in general unemployment and to provide work to those with impairments. Decisions concerning the willingness to use rehabilitation and training, as well as more direct intervention in the market—job subsidies, job creation, or job quotas—are central to the issue.

The final area concerns the degree to which a disability system should attempt to alter the socioeconomic structure of society to accommodate impaired citizens. To what degree should society be transformed so that impairments are made irrelevant to normal interactions? Policy decisions here determine the degree to which our society should be restructured to ensure "equal access" to all citizens. The major issues are: (1) to determine what equal access implies, (2) to assess the costs and benefits of providing equal access, and (3) to define the role government regulations should play in achieving equal access.

The Role of Insurance and Income Support within a Disability System

Government programs are often categorized as either insurance or welfare. This is a useful distinction in principle, but in fact programs are rarely entirely one or the other. Welfare programs focus on low-income people generally, and not on any particular low-income group such as the disabled. They are in general designed to achieve some level of social adequacy through income distribution. As discussed in chapter 2, the justification for state intervention to achieve this goal through welfare can be based on both efficiency and equity arguments. We have defined a primary element in the efficiency motivation as "collective compassion." Insurance programs, on the other hand, are meant to provide protection to individuals against an event whose occurrence cannot be predicted with certainty. In the case of disability, this uncertainty relates to the probability of a worker experiencing an impairment that entails a loss of earnings capacity. The justifications for state intervention to achieve this goal were also discussed in chapter 2; they are based primarily on efficiency arguments. While some income distribution may also occur in these programs, it is secondary to the purpose of reducing efficiency costs caused by market failure. Rather than consider all the differences between welfare and insurance programs, we focus here on the crucial difference between them—the relationship between contributions made into a program and subsequent benefits derived from it. In developing this contrast, we compare the strict insurance principles underlying most private disability programs to the structure of social insurance programs based on some combination of insurance and welfare objectives.

In most private disability programs, contributions are calculated on the basis of projected liabilities. That is, contributions are made either by individuals or by their employers at the level necessary to compensate some proportion of the losses of workers who become disabled. While benefits are not likely to equal actual payments for a given individual, the funding of a private pension program calls for contributions on behalf of a cohort of workers to cover the expected disability benefits of the group as a whole. The definition of an insured cohort is largely motivated to reduce information costs by enabling risk assignment to a fairly homogeneous group. Hence each cohort contains individuals with similar risks of becoming disabled. As a result, it is not surprising that many private disability insurance programs are developed for industry or occupational groups.

A welfare program, in contrast, is one in which benefits are divorced from contributions. Benefits are defined by law or regulation and are awarded on the basis of individual or family characteristics, such as income or family size. The recipient group here is based on societal attitudes about the characteristics upon which assistance should be targeted. The actual method of paying disability benefits is not critical in either type of program. Welfare benefits can be means-tested, as in the Supplemental Security Income (SSI) program, or they can be a flat amount based on the characteristics of the impairment (such as severity of impairment or medical expenses). Similarly, disability payments through a private insurance program can be provided in the form of an annuity or through a lump-sum benefit, again related to some characteristics of the impairment, such as the loss of a limb or eye.

The critical difference, then, is that in a program based on insurance principles, a worker's potential benefits are related to contributions made into the program by the individual or his or her employer. No such relation exists for a welfare program. In addition, the financing of an insurance program is based on a principle that imposes a balance between the expected present value of disability income and contributions for an individual or group. Welfare programs typically depend on general sources of financing.

A disability system of the insurance type will significantly affect the pattern in which net income is retained over an individual's lifetime. In effect, one is buying insurance against substantial losses in the event of disability. The cost of this protection is a yearly premium. Such a system, which bases benefits on contributions, will have the same effect on income distribution across individuals as that caused by private insurance. However, as discussed in chapter 2, this is the case only if private and public insurance are equally effective in overcoming the costs associated with assigning the risks of impairment. In the case of market failure, in which government intervention provided either a more or a less efficient method of providing insurance, income distribution will, of course, be affected. But this difference is a result of a more accurate assignment of risk, and is not an attempt to achieve a more equitable distribution of income. This is not the case with welfare programs based on equity or "collective compassion," which by their very nature strive to redistribute income, thus causing changes in the distribution of income both over an individual's lifetime and across individuals.

The Social Security Disability Insurance (DI) program—the cornerstone of income support policy toward the working-age disabled—is generally considered insurance, yet it clearly has many explicit welfare aspects. For instance, a worker who meets eligibility standards, regardless of previous wages or contributions into the system, is eligible for a minimum disability benefit. More importantly, the method of providing benefits offers higher benefits per dollar of contributions paid to low-wage workers and to workers with dependents. And no exact relation exists between benefits paid and incurred liabilities, since the system is "pay as you go." It is the tension between the insurance and welfare goals inherent in this program that is and will continue to be at the heart of much of the ongoing debate on disability income support policy.

The original Social Security Act of 1935 provided no coverage of the disabled population within the Social Security insurance program, but it did establish a limited federal commitment by providing welfare benefits to a small segment of the impaired population. This was done through federal grants to states for the Aid to the Blind (AB) and the Aid to the Permanently and Totally Disabled (APTD) programs. Because the United States had no general income support policy to aid people with low incomes, pressure to accommodate a wider welfare goal was brought to bear on the disability system. One result of this pressure was the introduction of the Supplemental Security Income (SSI) program in 1974. SSI protected all those previously eligible for AB and APTD by standardizing the minimum benefit requirements across states. But it also increased the level of benefits and the potential eligible population in most states. This was a major step in providing a welfare-based program to fully disabled people who either were ineligible for DI or for whom prior benefits were considered inadequate. This program places a "safety net" under the severely disabled. SSI bases benefits on needs, so those who are eligible for DI on health grounds but who lack a sufficient record of contributions to the Social Security system are nevertheless protected under SSI. It is significant that this program—unlike DI or the other two major disability insurance programs (Workers' Compensation, which provides protection based on a work record in a covered job, and Veterans' benefits, which provide eligibility based on service in the military)—breaks the link between market work and program eligibility. That is, the sharing of the costs of disability is based on a socially determined minimum income standard rather than on previous wage earnings.

90

The passage of the SSI program was a major expansion of the federal government's commitment to redistributing income based solely on humanitarian or moral grounds to those with low income within a disability context. The public policy justification of this development transcends the efficiency arguments based on market failure to justify work-related programs. It is also significant that in this program, benefits are related to a social commitment to assure some minimum income based solely on a health condition. However, SSI is a universal moral commitment neither to the poor nor to those in ill health since it, like DI, still attempts to separate the "qualified" impaired population—the totally disabled—from all other poor people. Hence it is of little help to those who are poor but not totally disabled or to those who are totally disabled but not poor.

The debate over the degree to which government should redistribute income through the disability system has been a continuous one. Those who favor an increase in the commitment to income redistribution have supported a broadening of the definition of a "qualified" impairment as a means of establishing a universal "safety net" for all poor people. The political commitment to such reform clearly varies with general economic conditions: it is no accident that the Social Security System itself was created in the midst of the Great Depression.

The pressure for increasing this redistribution commitment is exercised on two levels. The first is direct pressure on the government to increase explicitly the commitment of public programs to aid the disadvantaged. Proposals in this vein suggest relaxing the eligibility criteria of ongoing programs, increasing the benefit levels of these programs, or creating new programs. The second form of pressure involves increased utilization of current programs by the covered population or an administrative relaxation in enforcement of current program rules. It is this second type of pressure—reflected in increases in applications or acceptances—on which we focused in chapter 4.

This second type of pressure, which is related to the first, is more subtle. The dynamic may be something like this: Government increases the benefit levels or reduces the stringency of eligibility determinations of disability programs with both welfare and redistribution features. These changes are interpreted by those who view themselves as potentially eligible as a willingness of society to bear a greater share of the cost of disability. The potentially eligible in turn increase their efforts to gain access to the now more attractive program, and recipients and expenditures rise. To the extent that some of these individuals change their behavior in response to the program characteristics, a problem of "moral hazard" arises. Clearly, the more generous these programs, the greater the moral hazard problem.

The recognition that DI has a significant effect on work incentives—and that this effect is exacerbated by the income distribution features of the program—is likely to be the focal point of the debate over the future role of the program. This is especially so in light of the fact that SSI now reflects a major federal commitment to income distribution on equity grounds. Thus the thrust of the public policy debate in the 1980s in the area of income support programs is likely to center on the asserted need to continue to include specific welfare-related goals in the DI program. In considering this issue, it is useful to think about the political considerations that have influenced existing disability policy.

Historically social insurance programs have had substantially more public support than welfare programs. Because receipt of benefits from social insurance is less stigmatizing than receipt of welfare benefits, and because it has been easier to muster political support for increased social insurance benefits, these programs have been viewed as a superior means of aiding the poor. As a result, a program structure founded on insurance principles—justified on market failure grounds to protect against loss of income, but able to provide little help to the long-term poor—became a program serving a mixture of insurance and welfare goals.

The political value of tying income redistribution features to an insurance program was obvious to those who desired to increase the federal commitment to income distribution beyond that otherwise possible. But the costs of this dual insurance-welfare objective are also obvious, especially given the advent of SSI. As we have seen, the DI program generates both efficiency and administrative costs by seeking to serve both income redistributive and insurance goals. DI is financed by the use of a wage tax. The use of such a tax for an insurance system makes good sense. It can be thought of as a "user tax" in which liabilities are directly related to potential benefits. As a tax to redistribute income, however, it makes little sense. Because it is levied only on wage and salary incomes and only up to a maximum level, it tends to be regressive. It and the other Social Security payroll taxes now comprise the major share of taxes paid by most low- and middle-income people. Using such revenues to support income distribution goals seems clearly perverse. This is especially the case now that SSI (which is funded by general tax revenues) guarantees "safety net" protection against poverty, but little more, even if supplanted by DI. Because of this guarantee, the OASDI taxes paid by low-income workers yield them little or nothing in the way of additional benefits.

As a result, a reduction in the payroll tax together with a matching increase in SSI benefits would clearly maintain the "collective compassion" commitment of society. It would at the same time more equitably distribute its burden. In addition, such a change would allow DI to more closely follow insurance principles.

A possible approach in broadening the coverage of the SSI program would be to relax its current health restrictions. In this case, the program would become a more general income support program for any poor person with a longer-term health problem. An important implication of this would be that the DI program could be altered so as to emphasize its insurance function by reducing its reliance on vocational eligibility criteria and its pro-poor tilt in benefits.[1]

Given the change in administration, it is not likely that the traditional pattern of incremental expansions of the DI program—expansions that increased its income distribution role—will be pursued in the early 1980s. The new administration has suggested a quite different approach: elimination of the vocational criteria in eligibility determination, an increase in the waiting period, and a general reduction in the income support role of the DI program through an adjustment of the benefit structure. These changes, if brought about, would eliminate access to the DI program for low-skill, low-education, and older workers with some impairment. This group, as we have emphasized, has accounted for much of the past decade's growth in disability roles and expenditures.

If the administration's proposals are adopted, some of the disadvantaged or marginal workers will be able to continue in the labor force, and a reduction in the DI commitment to these workers will increase otherwise lost productivity. However, many of these workers are unlikely to qualify for private insurance benefits, and many will be unable to continue working. It is unclear what protection public policy will provide them under the proposals of the new administration. Clearly, part of the "collective compassion" effort will be taken up by nongovernment sources. In the absence of public support people have traditionally banded together and extended their network of moral responsibility through family units, religious organizations, trade unions, and private charities, and to some extent such private collective action will replace public programs. Whether the new administration will rely solely on such private responses, or, in their absence, will allow income support to impaired marginally employable citizens to erode is unclear.

The Role of Disability Policy
in Achieving Employment Objectives

In addition to considering issues regarding the extent to which the disability system should support the incomes of disabled people, and the means of providing that support, policymakers must also consider the relationship of disability policy to employment policy. This section deals with some of the relationships of disability and employment policies, and raises a number of issues that must, in some way, be resolved as policy evolves.

Income Transfers and Work

Since the SSI and DI programs offer some income protection to those workers most susceptible to unemployment during economic downturns—older workers, the impaired, or the unskilled—the demands for program benefits increase during recessions. Moreover, as the standards for disability eligibility have been lowered to include work-related characteristics, the sensitivity of these programs to market conditions has increased. And, as the share of an individual's costs of disability borne by these programs increases, the alternatives to continued work or job search become more attractive. Thus the disability income support system has played an important role in removing from the labor force—and hence from unemployment rolls—those older, low-skilled workers found least productive in a slack economy.[2]

The degree to which disability income support programs should be used by government to encourage the early retirement of older, impaired workers is likely to become an important public policy question during the next decade. Currently most workers are covered by Unemployment Insurance. However, these benefits typically end after twenty-six weeks. During periods of high unemployment benefits are extended, but even under these conditions benefits usually last no longer than thirty-nine weeks. One policy alternative to relying on continually expanding general unemployment insurance is to use disability income support programs as a means of dealing with long-term unemployment. In fact, in some industrialized countries, long-term unemployment is a sufficient condition for eligibility to disability programs. Especially for workers who are difficult to reemploy (for example, the aged and impaired, or those with low skills), disability programs are increasingly seen as a means of extending unemployment benefits—or, more accurately, providing early retirement benefits—to those not "expected" to work by society.

In this country the use of the Social Security system as part of a general government strategy to reduce unemployment has a long history. The debate over its establishment took place in the midst of the Great Depression, and the rhetoric of that debate reflects the political value of using retirement benefits to reduce the labor supply and hence unemployment of older workers. Indeed, it is difficult to understand the anti-work bias of the dollar-for-dollar earnings test of the early Social Security retirement program without recognizing the importance assigned to it as a means of reducing measured unemployment.

A continuation of this same public policy debate is now shaping up. Its outcome will determine the degree to which disability programs continue to be relied upon as a means of reducing unemployment. As a part of its overall reform of the Social Security system, the current administration has suggested a major increase in the total benefits available for postponing the receipt of Social Security retirement benefits to age 65.[3] An alternative proposal[4] would postpone full benefit eligibility to age 68 while reducing benefits at age 62 by 36 percent. Both proposals are likely to have an important effect on work behavior, and both would relieve the existing cost pressure on OASI. Unfortunately, most of the discussion of these options has centered on their cost-saving impact; little attention has been given to their overall affect on either general employment or welfare policy.

There is little question that the availability of Social Security retirement benefits at age 62 has reduced the work effort of older men. And arguments can be made that a change in this policy is desirable. While postponement of retirement age is one possible change, any such proposal must recognize that a postponement of retirement age will place pressure on other programs, especially the DI and SSI programs. Many

95

older workers who are retired could and would work in the absence of OASI. Any reduction in early retirement benefits under OASI would be a further inducement for workers to attempt to use DI as an alternative "early retirement" program. This would be especially true for a worker with some impairment who was unemployed and who had exhausted unemployment benefits. Hence, attempts to reduce the cost of a single program must be put in the broader context of its full effect on all program costs.

The proposals of the current administration do implicitly recognize this interaction; they propose that the DI eligibility criteria be tightened. As noted, however, without some adjustments in SSI eligibility requirements or benefits, private institutions—families, charities—would be expected to assist disadvantaged, long-term unemployed workers. No explicit government programs to employ these workers have been considered. The position of the government is that the expanded employment forthcoming from its macroeconomic policies will remove pressure on all income support programs, including DI and SSI. The accuracy of this assessment remains to be demonstrated.

Rehabilitation and Job Creation

The federal government has long espoused a policy of increasing the ability of disabled workers to overcome their impairments through rehabilitation and job training. However, the resources committed to this effort have been far fewer than those committed to income support. Our review of rehabilitation programs suggested that they were principally motivated as an attempt either to reduce overall income support costs or to increase productivity. In calculating the benefits and costs of these efforts, little weight was given to the sociopsychological benefits of work. Nevertheless, evaluations of these programs appear to show that they did succeed, even within this narrowly framed benefit-cost account.

The reluctance to employ rehabilitation efforts as more than a cost-reducing mechanism is in sharp contrast to the attitude of many other industrialized countries, where the sociopsychological benefits of work are given great weight, and where rehabilitation and job placement dominate disability policy. In these countries, protection for the disabled has almost always been provided within the context of a protected job (or at least preparation for such a job) which the government would supply either directly or through the use of subsidies or quotas. Indeed, much of the debate in the United States over income transfers versus employment efforts is not loudly heard in Europe. There is little hesitation by these governments to intervene directly in the general economy to provide jobs for disabled workers.

Because of the emphasis on income support rather than job creation, United States policy toward the working-age disabled has contained a number of contradictions. The DI program, for example, imposes a severe earnings test while at the same time directing substantial funds to the rehabilitation of beneficiaries. The SSI program taxes away 50 percent of additional earnings (beyond an initial $65) and 100 percent of Social Security benefits, while the Vocational Rehabilitation Program is simultaneously working with SSI beneficiaries in an attempt to return them to the labor force. Sheltered workshops receive government support for some of their activities, but in some cases they are exempted from minimum-wage laws, permitting them to pay wage rates that often fail to exceed $1 per hour. Further, all of these discouragements to work exist in the face of demands made by the handicapped that they should be given equal access to employment opportunities.

Yet in the late 1960s and 1970s the employment of the disabled began to fall. As the economy fared badly during this period, so too did disabled workers. They were more expendable than nondisabled workers and lost out in competition with them. Levitan and Taggert (1977) estimate that between 1966 and 1972, severely and occupationally disabled males aged 20 to 64 who were not in the labor force increased from 38 to 50 percent of the total group, while the percentage employed decreased from 56 to 50 percent. Also during this period the success of the vocational rehabilitation program fell; the ratio of successful to unsuccessful closure rates fell from 3.4 during the period from 1965 to 1968 to 2.3 in 1975. While it is likely that macroeconomic performance accounts for much of this decrease in employment, benefits in disability programs were also expanding during this period and eligibility requirements were being relaxed.

Given the demographic and economic characteristics of the disabled, no substantial reversal in this declining employment-increased transfer recipiency pattern is to be expected, even if the administration's proposals to diminish replacement rates, reduce work disincentives, and tighten eligibility standards are adopted. These changes in the income maintenance system will lower the inducement for the handicapped not to work. But unless rehabilitation and job-training services are available for many disabled people whose market skills are not sufficient for them to compete successfully, work will not be possible. Indeed, even with the provision of such services, disabled workers are unlikely to register major employment gains without policy measures that would directly stimulate the demand for their services. This is especially so in the face of the rapid growth in the labor force participation rates of youth and women.

Direct intervention in the labor market has always been a controversial policy in the United States, and this is one reason for the emphasis on income support rather than jobs for the disabled. In the mid-1970s, however, two pieces of legislation were enacted which, implicitly at least, argued that government must have a role in directly stimulating the demand for less productive, including handicapped, workers if their employment is to increase. The first of these demand-side measures is included in the Rehabilitation Act of 1973, which requires government agencies and contractors to have an Affirmative Action Program for employing and advancing disabled workers. The second is the Targeted Jobs Tax Credit described in chapter 5. It provides private employers up to $3,000 of first-year-salary support for hiring disabled workers referred by vocational rehabilitation agencies.

These measures, then, which were only implemented by the late 1970s, can be considered as first steps toward direct government intervention designed to encourage the employment of disabled workers. A wide range of additional demand-side measures have also been proposed. These include public service employment for disabled workers, direct employment and salary subsidies to sheltered workshops, and legislated employment quotas for private businesses.

Yet the employment potential of all these measures is largely untested, and the prospective costs for some of them are great. Nevertheless, substantial support for expansion of such direct job-creation measures is provided by disabled groups favoring the integration of disabled workers into the economy. In addition, taxpayers are likely to prefer employment provision to cash transfers. Again, study of the net job-creation impacts of these measures per dollar of cost is in order prior to full-scale implementation of any of them.

Complementary to efforts to stimulate the demand for disabled workers, but much less controversial, are recent policy changes designed to reduce the work disincentives in existing income transfer legislation. Concern with this issue is reflected in the 1980 amendments to the Social

Security Disability Insurance program. These amendments change the emphasis of the DI program in several ways; they either reduce disincentives to work currently incorporated in the program or provide positive inducements for work and leaving the DI rolls. The issue of high replacement rates is addressed directly by the placing of a cap on the total monthly benefit to which any recipient is entitled. While the definition of the cap is complicated, its intent is to restrict total benefits to no more than 85 percent of the individual's average indexed monthly earnings. In addition, the amendments also change the program to allow certain work-related expenses attributable to severe disability to be deducted from earnings in evaluating the SGA provision. Because of this, earnings in excess of $300 per month may not exclude recipients from continued benefits. Further, the amendments permit the receipt of Medicare benefits to continue for an additional three years beyond the twelve-month trial work period. This provision is to counter the concern that workers who are successful during the trial work period may nevertheless return to recipiency status after the trial period in order to avoid the loss of medical benefits.

The evidence suggests that major increases in the employment of those currently receiving disability benfits is not likely without major intervention into the private sector. However, increased rehabilitation efforts should have some impact, especially on younger disabled workers. As for disadvantaged workers who are older, unskilled, and have little education, no easy solutions are likely. Clearly Social Security retirement and disability programs have been used to offer such workers an "early retirement" option. These workers would not qualify for disability benefits under a stricter health-related disability system, yet their market skills make it likely that they would experience high levels of unemployment. Unless significant improvement in overall economic conditions occur, they will be in need of some alternative income support program. This issue is one of the most important to be resolved in the disability policy area in the 1980s.

The Role of "Equal Access" in a Disability System

Direct demand-side intervention in the labor market during the 1970s moved the government into a new role in trying to integrate the disabled into the economy of work. While this new initiative signified a major change, it has been accompanied by an even more drastic integration

99

effort. Also beginning in the 1970s, the government has moved toward guaranteeing the disabled "equal access" to education, employment, and mobility. By declaring that living in a barrier-free environment is a fundamental "right" of disabled people, the government for the first time stated its intent to adjust social norms to accommodate the handicapped, rather than to provide assistance to the handicapped in their efforts to adjust to social norms.

This commitment to such a major structural change signaled a radical new element in disability policy, an element first supported by political action groups of the handicapped population. While these groups defined the equal access issue, by the end of the 1970s the government itself accepted the proposition that handicapped people should be assured of full integration into the productive processes of society. Using the civil rights legislation of the 1960s as a model, the government—through legislation in the 1970s—guaranteed handicapped people "equal opportunity" in employment and education, and "equal access" to all public facilities. As a means of sharing or reducing the costs of disability, this new approach goes well beyond income support or rehabilitation, or even direct job creation. The crucial issue on which the debate over this approach must focus is the costs of this strategy to the nondisabled relative to the benefits conveyed to the disabled.

This area of public policy debate poses serious moral and legal questions. The principle of "equal access" and subsequent legal attempts to define it are based on the experiences of the civil rights movement of the 1960s. Few criticize the goals espoused in such civil rights rhetoric. But there are major differences between preventing discrimination against racial and sexual groups and providing equal access to the handicapped. The primary difference concerns the social and taxpayer costs of this provision in comparison to its benefits. Clearly, if the provision of equal access to, say, public transportation facilities would lead to a substantial increase in ridership by the handicapped, and, in turn, increased employment, income and social activities of this group, diversion of nontrivial amounts of society's resources could be justified. However, if these gains did not occur, attainment of the "equal access" goal would have to serve as an inviolable principle. The question then is: What is the cost required to attain "equal access," and are these costs less than the value of achieving this goal?

As suggested, the costs of assuring equal access to the handicapped are likely to be of a different magnitude than the costs of assuring equal opportunity to racial minorities and women. Equality of treatment by sex and race does not require adapted workplaces, specialized machines, specialized training, altered cafeteria and toilet facilities, alternative means for building entry and movement between floors. While discrimination plays a role in employment, education, and mobility decisions regarding both the handicapped and the racial and sexual groups, the relative contribution of such attitudes toward the unequal status of the handicapped would seem to be substantially smaller than in the case of the latter groups. Conversely, the real costs of securing true equal opportunity for the handicapped are likely to be substantially higher. At the present time the magnitude of these costs is unknown and, in essence, will depend critically on the regulatory decisions that are made in this area, and on how they are enforced. Conversely, making efficient decisions regarding the enforcement of this regulatory legislation requires knowledge of the aggregate costs associated with various levels of regulatory stringency.

In chapter 5 we illustrated the difficult choices confronted in this area by describing the Transbus controversy. We emphasized the need for some process that would insure that both the costs and the benefits of various enforcement options become reflected in the decisions made if serious resource misallocations were to be avoided. While the need for such a decision-making mechanism would appear to be required primarily by efficiency concerns, it should be noted that an important equity issue lurks slightly beneath the surface. While some social programs targeted at a group tend to benefit all members of the group equally, other social programs targeted at a group may benefit certain subgroups substantially more than others. Similarly, policy choices among various accessibility options are likely to convey substantially different benefits to subgroups among the disabled. The degree and type of impairment are likely to be important variables. Analyses of benefits and costs of various accessibility options must proceed one step further; they must distinguish who among the handicapped will be helped or hurt by a move to higher or lower levels of access. Again, resolution of these efficiency and equity issues is likely to be central in the evolution of disability policy in the 1980s.

In this volume we separated the coming public debate over disability policy into three potential areas of conflict: income support, employment, and equal access. We then attempted to develop an economic perspective for society's treatment of handicapped people based on the principles discussed in chapter 2. But it should be clear that operationalizing these concepts and defining the socially acceptable share of disability costs to be borne by taxpayers depends first on the development of an overall view of the optimal level of government intervention in society and the role disability programs should play in this intervention. Hence, it must first be recognized that disability income support or employment policy is really only a subset economy-wide income support or employment policy. Similarly, the regulatory nature of equal access legislation is a subset of a broader use of regulation to alter market processes.

Each of these areas of disability policy on which debate will be focused affects the other. A strong equal access program, for example, could no doubt reduce the costs of both income support and job subsidy programs. Similarly, a strong disability income support system would make superfluous many job-support and equal-access goals.

The final mix of programs, then, will depend on the share of costs society is willing to remove from handicapped people, as well as on notions regarding the most efficient and equitable means of sharing this burden. In the coming debate on the level and type of disability assistance, it should be recognized that those who emphasize jobs for the disabled cannot claim that such jobs dominate income transfers on efficiency grounds. Rather, it is a stronger commitment to a "full employment" goal—defined as the availability of a job to any citizen who wants one—and a willingness to bear the associated costs that distinguishes such job advocates from those who reject this strategy. Thus the debate will not be decided on cost-reducing grounds, but on some social judgment regarding the size and configuration of public intervention that must be imposed by the political process. The same is even more true as regards the "equal access" issue. In the past, while lip service was paid to work-related programs for the disabled, the commitment to the disabled effectively ended with income support.

The overriding disability policy issue in the 1980s, then, concerns the willingness of society to share the costs of disability, or to undertake investments to reduce these costs. The initial battles over disability policy will signal what the new level of commitment will be as well as what configuration of policies will be undertaken to reach that level. It appears as if the era of Social Security policy based on the premise that "a little bit more is always a good thing and anything less is inconceivable" may be replaced by an older tradition, one based on the premises that government intervention does not always yield benefits commensurate with costs, and that a search for those cases in which it does is in order.

Appendixes

Appendix A. Characteristics of Major Programs Affecting the Working-Age Disabled

	Social Security Disability Insurance	Supplemental Security Income	Workers' Compensation	Veterans' Compensation and Pension
Eligibility requirements	Physical or mental impairment causing inability to engage in substantial gainful activity. Impairment is to last for twelve months or result in death. Unable to engage in substantial gainful activity for at least five months at time of claim. Medical evidence from doctor, hospital, agency, or institution concerning physical conditions and medical history. Employment or self-employment covered by the Social Security program for at least one-half of the forty quarters prior to onset of disability. Self-employed persons contributing to Social Security program.	Physical or mental impairment lasting twelve months or resulting in death. Medical evidence from doctor, hospital, agency, or institution concerning physical condition and medical history. Income must not exceed $189.40/mo. ($2,273/yr.) for a single person and $284.10/mo. ($3,409/yr.) for a couple. Persons in institutions receive reduced benefits. Medically determined alcoholics and drug addicts must accept treatment. Must accept services offered for vocational rehabilitation.	Temporary or permanent work-related injury, disease or death. Employed by an employer subjected to or voluntarily abiding by the state's WC act.	*Veterans' Compensation:* Disability incurred or aggravated in line of U.S. military service (need not be recognized at time of release or discharge) and limits earnings capacity. Active wartime service without a dishonorable discharge. Dependent of veterans with wartime service with a minimum of 50% disability (as defined by the Veterans' Administration). *Veterans' Pension:* Active wartime service without a dishonorable discharge. Disability that is not necessarily service-connected and limits earnings capacity. Income must not exceed $3,000/yr. for a single person and $4,200/yr. for a couple. Aged 65 or older with wartime service.

106

	Same as column 1.	Disability rated in intervals from 10% to 100% by Veterans Administration board based on medical evidence and using the VA's detailed Schedule for Rating Disabilities.
Satisfy certain "objective" impairment conditions detailed in a standard list recognized as severe disabilities.	Work-related impairment must satisfy state specific statutory definitions and tests.	Ratings are made according to average loss of earnings capacity.
Or, for persons who have been engaged in arduous unskilled employment for a long period of time, presenting evidence that impairments prevent them from engaging in such work.	Or, work-related impairment meets state specific list of "scheduled injuries" which specifies predetermined benefits.	
Or, demonstrating through examination of a person's functional capacity, age, education, and training, demands of his/her customary work; and work availability that he/she is unable to work.	State-based claims board or commission which determines eligibility based on above definitions and schedules.	
Appeal and judicial review Reconsideration through normal case determination procedures.	Same as column 1.	
Secondly, hearing before an administrative law judge of the SSA.	Reviewing boards are provided in many states within the WC commission.	
Thirdly, review of hearing decision by the Appeals Court of the SSA.	Further appeals, or original appeals in states without receiving boards, generally handled through courts.	
Finally, present case in a federal court.		

Appendix A. *(continued)*

Size of population being served and its growth

Social Security Disability Insurance	Supplemental Security Income	Workers' Compensation	Veterans' Compensation and Pension
Disabled Workers and Dependents:	Number of recipients (1978): 2,171,890.	Number of recipients (1975): 1,249,640.	*All Ages:*
Number of recipients (1978): 4,868,576.	Number of recipients as a percentage of working-age population (1978): 1.7%.	Number of recipients as a percentage of working-age population (1975): 1.0%.	Number of recipients (1978): 3,286,000.
Number of recipients as a percentage of working-age population (1978): 3.8%.	Number of recipients as a percentage of employed population (1978): 2.3%.	Number of recipients as a percentage of employed population (1975): 1.5%.	Number of recipients as a percentage of working-age population (1978): 2.5%.
Number of recipients as a percentage of employed population (1978): 5.2%.	Number of recipients (1968): 703,000.	Number of recipients (1968): 870,000.	Number of recipients as a percentage of employed population (1978): 3.5%.
Number of recipients (1968): 2,335,134.	Number of recipients as a percentage of working-age population (1968): 0.65%.	Number of recipients as a percentage of working-age population (1968): 0.81%.	Number of recipients (1968): 3,164,000.
Number of recipients as a percentage of working-age population (1968): 2.2%.	Number of recipients as a percentage of employed population (1968): 0.33%.	Number of recipients as a percentage of employed population (1968): 1.0%.	Number of recipients as a percentage of working-age population (1968): 2.9%.
Number of recipients as a percentage of employed population (1958): 3.1%.	Average annual growth of number of recipients (1968 to 1978): 11.9%.	Average annual growth of number of recipients (1968 to 1978): 3.7%.	Number of recipients as a percentage of employed population (1968): 4.2%.
Average annual growth of number of recipients (1968 to 1978): 7.6%.			Average annual growth of number of recipients (1968 to 1978): 0.4%.

Disabled Workers Only:

Number of recipients (1978): 2,879,828.

Number of recipients as a percentage of working-age population (1978): 2.2%.

Number of recipients as a percentage of employed population (1978): 3.1%.

Number of recipients (1968): 1,295,300.

Number of recipients as a percentage of working-age population (1968): 1.2%.

Number of recipients as a percentage of employed population (1968): 1.7%.

Average annual growth of number of recipients (1968 to 1978): 8.3%.

Program expenditures (1978, millions of current dollars): $12,513 (1978, millions of 1967 dollars): $6,407.

Program expenditures (1978, millions of current dollars): $4,049 (1978, millions of 1967 dollars): $2,073.

Younger than 65:

Number of recipients (1978): 2,490,000.

Number of recipients as a percentage of working-age population (1978): 1.9%.

Number of recipients as a percentage of employed population (1978): 2.6%.

Number of recipients (1968): 2,138,000.

Number of recipients as a percentage of working-age population (1968): 2.0%.

Number of recipients as a percentage of employed population (1968): 2.8%.

Average annual growth of number of recipients (1968 to 1978): 1.5%.

Program expenditures (1978, millions of current dollars): $8,400 (1978, millions of 1967 dollars): $4,301.

Program expenditures (1978, millions of current dollars): $7,000 (1978, millions of 1967 dollars): $3,584.

Program Expenditures

109

Appendix A. *(continued)*

	Social Security Disability Insurance	Supplemental Security Income	Workers' Compensation	Veterans' Compensation and Pension
Program expenditures	Program expenditures as a percentage of total government expenditures (1978): 1.9%; as a percentage of federal expenditures (1978): 2.8%.	Program expenditures as a percentage of total government expenditures (1975): 0.52%; as a percentage of federal expenditures (1978): 0.75%.	Program expenditures as a percentage of total government expenditures (1978): 1.8%; as a percentage of federal expenditures (1978): 1.9%.	Program expenditures as a percentage of total government expenditures (1978): 1.1%; as a percentage of federal expenditures 1.6%.
	Program expenditures (1968, millions of current dollars): $2,088 (1968, millions of 1967 dollars): $2,004. *	Program expenditures (1968, millions of current dollars): $656 (1968, millions of 1967 dollars): $639.	Program expenditures (1968, millions of current dollars): $2,366 (1968 millions of 1967 dollars): $2,271.	Program expenditures (1968, millions of current dollars): $3,265 (1968, millions of 1967 dollars): $3,133.
	Program expenditures as a percentage of total government expenditures (1968): 0.72%; as a percentage of federal expenditures (1968): 1.2%.	Program expenditures as a percentage of total government expenditures (1968): 0.23%; as a percentage of federal expenditures (1968): 0.38%.	Program expenditures as a percentage of total government expenditures (1968): 0.8%; as a percentage of federal expenditures (1968): 1.4%.	Program expenditures as a percentage of total government expenditures (1968): 1.1%; as a percentage of federal government expenditures (1968): 1.9%.
	Average annual growth of program expenditures (1968 to 1978, current dollars): 19.6% (1968 to 1978, 1967 dollars): 12.3%.	Average annual growth of program expenditures (1968 to 1978, current dollars): 20% (1968 to 1978, 1967 dollars): 12.5%.	Average annual growth of program expenditures (1968 to 1978, current dollars): 13.5% (1968 to 1978, 1967 dollars): 6.6%.	Average annual growth of program expenditures (1968 to 1978, current dollars): 7.9% (1968 to 1978, 1967 dollars): 1.4%.
	SSI: eligible for SSI benefits if DI benefits plus outside income (and a given asset measure) fail to meet a specified minimum-income standard.	Benefits decline on a dollar-for-dollar basis against any nonlabor income, including other disability program benefits, after a $240 per year disregard.	DI: Reduction in DI benefit when DI benefit plus Workers' Compensation benefit exceeds 80% of the workers' average current earnings.	Ninety percent of Social Security and other disability pension income is counted as income in calculation of veterans' pension benefit.

Integration with other programs			
WC: Reduces DI benefit when DI benefit plus WC benefit exceeds 80 percent of the workers' average current earnings. Vocational Rehabilitation: Application for DI benefits entitles application to vocational rehabiliation services; beneficiaries may receive services as well. Medicare: Eligible for Medicare benefits during coverage under DI program if covered (or eligible for coverage) for at least twenty-four months. Private Disability Insurance: Private programs frequently reduce benefits dollar for dollar against DI up to total DI benefit level; private benefits may supplement the DI benefits beyond this level. Other Social Security Benefits: Entitlement to more than one benefit, for example, disability and retirement, typically results in receiving the largest of the benefits.	DI: Supports low-income DI recipients' benefit levels and acts as an alternate channel of support for persons failing to qualify for DI due to lack of insured status. Medicaid: Generally eligible for Medicaid benefits while covered under SSI. WC: Supports low-income WC recipients' benefit levels and acts as an alternate channel of support for persons whose benefits run out.	SSI: May be used to supplement Workers' Compensation benefit if WC plus outside income and assets value fall below a certain minimum level. State Vocational Rehabilitation: most states provide rehabilitation provision in WC laws.	Disabled veterans are provided free medical care through the Veterans' Administration Medical system (hospitals, outpatient clinics, nursing homes and domiciliaries) for service- and nonservice-connected disabilities. Widows and dependents are also eligible for care through the VA medical system.

Appendix A. *(continued)*

	Social Security Disability Insurance	Supplemental Security Income	Workers' Compensation	Veterans' Compensation and Pension
Procedures for Termination	Upon reaching age 65 recipient is automatically transferred from DI to retired-worker status. Benefits remain the same.	Upon reaching age 65 recipient is automatically transferred from SSI disability to SSI aged. Benefits remain the same.	Automatic termination results upon reaching state time limit, irrespective of disability status.	
	Recipient must notify SSA any time medical evidence shows recovery from disability; benefits will continue to be sent for three months from time of recovery.	Recipient must notify SSA of changes in status that affect SSI payments, such as any changes in income, living arrangements, marriage status.	Otherwise benefits are terminated upon returning to initial working status.	
	Trial work plan enables beneficiary to return to work while disabled and continue to receive benefits for a period of nine months; if work is SGA, then benefits discontinue three months after trial period.	Recipient must notify SSA at any time medical evidence shows recovery from disability.		
	Beneficiary must notify the SSA if returning to work irrespective of change in condition or amount of earnings.	Redeterminations are made periodically to make certain recipient is still eligible.		

Program Turnover	An estimated 3.3% of recipients left the rolls in 1967 because of recovery, and 1.6% left through recovery in 1976.			
Financing Program	Funds raised through the Social Security payroll tax: a small amount of disability funds is maintained in a trust fund independent of the other SSA program funds, but the system is pay-as-you-go financed. Payroll taxes are collected at a rate (1978) of 0.775% for both employees and employers for the employees' first $17,000 of earnings; increasing to 0.65% and $29,700 in 1981. Self-employed persons pay taxes at the slightly higher rate of 0.109% in 1978 and 0.975% in 1981.	Financed from general funds of the U.S. Treasury.	Varies by employer and influenced by state requirements. Generally one of three financing (insuring) channels is established: 1. self-insurance, that is, financed through internal revenues, 2. insurance through a private insurance company, or 3. insurance through a state-operated fund established solely to provide workers' compensation insurance.	General Veterans Administration funds.

SOURCES: Disability Insurance: U.S. Department of Health, Education, and Welfare, Social Security Administration (1977), (1978b), and (1978c). Supplemental Security Income: U.S. Department of Health, Education, and Welfare, Social Security Administration (1978a), and conversations with Social Security Administration representatives. Workers' Compensation: Chamber of Commerce of the United States (1968) and (1978), and conversations with National Council on Compensation Insurance (NCCI) representatives. Veterans' Compensation and Pension: U.S. Department of Health and Human Services, Social Security Administration (1981a) and (1981b), and Ladinsky (1977). Expenditure data: See table 3.1. Recipients' data: U.S. Department of Health, Education, and Welfare, Social Security Administration (1977), (1979a), (1979b), and (1979c); U.S. Department of Health and Human Services (1981a) and (1981b).

Appendix B. Additional Public Programs Providing Income Support or Services to the Working-Age Disabled

Program[a]	Allocation of Program Expenditure to the Working-Age Disabled (as a percentage)[b]	Total Program Expenditures, 1977 ($ millions)[c]	Expenditures Allocated to the Working-Age Disabled, 1977 ($ millions)
1. Aid to families with dependent children	20	11,100	2,220
2. Federal civil service employees' sick leave	100	1,173*	1,173
3. Federal Employees' Compensation Act	100	589	589
4. Longshoremen's and Harbor Workers' Act	100	6	6
5. Food Stamp Program	32	5,474	1,752
6. Veterans Administration Hospitals	100	2,862	2,862
7. Civilian Health and Medical Program of the Uniform Services (CHAMPUS)	100	556*	556
8. General hospital and medical care	100	6,729*	6,729
9. Social service to public assistance recipients	30	3,527	1,058
10. Veterans' dependents educational assistance	27	210	57
11. Veterans Administration alcohol and drug dependency	100	107	107
12. Adapted housing for disabled veterans	100	14	14
13. Adapted Autos for Disabled Veterans	100	14	14
14. U.S. Soldiers and Airmen's Home	100	16	16
15. Medical Services and Captioned Film Loan	100	17*	17
16. NIH Drug Abuse Community Service	100	159	159
17. Drug Abuse Formula Grants	100	22*	22
18. NIH Alcohol Abuse Grants	100	56	56
19. Federal Employment Service	20	614	123

Program [a]	Allocation of Program Expenditure to the Working-Age Disabled (as a percentage) [b]	Total Program Expenditures, 1977 ($ millions) [c]	Expenditures Allocated to the Working-Age Disabled, 1977 ($ millions)
20. Gallaudet College	100	18*	18
21. National Technical Institute for the Deaf	100	9*	9
22. American Printing Housing for the Blind	100	2*	2
23. Books for the Blind and Handicapped	100	12*	12
24. Cooperative extension services	5	388*	19
25. State Compulsory Temporary Disability Insurance	100	1,016*	1,016
26. General assistance	50	1,200	600
27. State and Local Employees' Sick Leave	100	2,374*	2,374
28. Compulsory Temporary Disability Insurance	100	93	93
29. General assistance—medical	88	142*	125
30. Blind Veterans Rehabilitation Centers	100	3	3
31. Community Nursing Home Care for Veterans	100	75	75
32. Comprehensive Services Support	50	132	66
33. Emergency assistance	20	120	24
34. Handicapped Assistance Loans	100	13	13
35. Housing for the Elderly and Handicapped	30	262	79
36. Veterans Contract Hospitalization	100	55	55
37. Veterans Domiciliary Care	100	69	69

(continued)

Appendix B. *(continued)*

	Program[a]	*Allocation of Program Expenditure to the Working-Age Disabled (as a percentage)* [b]	*Total Program Expenditures, 1977 ($ millions)* [c]	*Expenditures Allocated to the Working-Age Disabled, 1977 ($ millions)*
38.	Veterans Grants for State Home Care	100	36	36
39.	Veterans Nursing Home Care	100	147	147
40.	Veterans Outpatient Care	100	872	872
41.	Veterans Prescription Service	100	12	12
42.	Veterans Prosthetic Appliances	100	50	50
	Total			23,287

SOURCES:

[a]Programs numbered 1–31 are taken from the list of relevant programs in Bureau of Economic Research, Rutgers University (1975). Programs numbered 32–44 were identified as relevant from W. J. Lawrence and S. Leeds (1978).

[b]The allocation percentages for programs 1–31 are taken from Bureau of Economic Research, Rutgers University (1975). See the rationale for each percentage presented there. The allocation percentages for programs 32–44 are "guesstimates" in part based on DHER rationale, and are believed to be conservative. A revised and somewhat lower percentage of the benefits of the medical-care-related programs is allocated to the working-age disabled in Monroe Berkowitz and David Dean (1980).

[c]Those program expenditure estimates carrying an asterisk are upward adjustments from the 1973 estimates presented in Bureau of Economic Research, Rutgers University (1975). The adjustment assumes that expenditures for each program grew by 7 percent per year from 1973 to 1977. The remaining estimates are from W. J. Lawrence and S. Leeds (1978).

Notes

Chapter 1

1. See Hodgens (1975).
2. In this volume the terms *impairment, disability*, and *handicap* are used as they are conceptually defined by Nagi (1979). In these definitions, disability is recognized as a limitation on the performing of tasks that society has come to expect of individuals. Therefore, it is the outcome of a combination of impairments and social expectations. For a discussion on the difficulties in defining and measuring *impairment* and *disability*, see Garrad (1974).

Chapter 2

1. Disability was defined as "a limitation in the kind or amount of work (or housework) resulting from a chronic health condition or impairment lasting three or more months." This definition, it should be noted, differs from that employed by the Social Security Administration for establishing eligibility for Disability Insurance or Supplemental Security Income-Disability benefits. These program-related definitions are discussed later. In using this definition, we are able to distinguish among various work-related degrees of impairment in estimating a disabled population. *Severely disabled* implies an inability to work altogether or regularly. *Occupationally disabled* indicates an inability to do the same work as one was doing before the onset of the disability, or an inability to work full time. *Secondary work limitations* indicate limitations in the performance of work, even if full-time and regular work of the same type occur. See Allan (1976), pp. 19, 35, and Riley and Nagi (1970), p. 1.
2. However, when age was controlled for, education attainment was still found to be significantly associated with disability. See Lando (1975), pp. 18–20, and Wolfe (1980).
3. Clearly, age, race, and education are not unrelated characteristics. Being black, for example, increases the probability that one will have fewer years of education. Lando and Krute report that standardizing for age and education simultaneously explains 63 percent of the racial differences for men and 28 percent of the racial differences for women. See Lando and Krute (1976), p. 4, and Lando (1975).

117

4. One other point should be made about the economic status of the disabled. Ultimately, an accurate measure of the economic status of the disabled must rest on a concept of "full income" (see Oi, 1977). The full income of a person can be defined as the value of his or her total time endowment which can be used for work or leisure, and his or her nonearned income. Given this definition, there are a number of ways in which a person's health or disability status can affect his or her full income. First, because a disabled person typically needs a larger number of hours per week for "maintenance" than does a nondisabled person, an impairment reduces the number of hours available for work or leisure, hence reducing full income. Second, an impairment tends to reduce the wage rate that a person's productivity can command. And because this wage rate is used to value both labor and leisure hours, full income is again decreased. Third, it can be shown that the reduction in the disabled person's productivity and wage rate will bring about a reduction in labor supply, labor force participation, and, hence, earned income as well. Although no data have been presented on the economic status of the disabled relative to the nondisabled in terms of full income, it seems clear that the full-income concept, which incorporates time as a scarce resource, is more appropriate for defining economic status than is the realized money (or money plus in-kind) income concept. The notion of disability-required "maintenance" time in reducing full income is an important one and, if the full-income concept could be measured, might well lead to the conclusion that full-income disparities between the disabled and the nondisabled are even larger than the observed disparities in money income shown here.

5. Indeed, if the sizable proportion of severely disabled persons not reporting weekly earnings had done so, this disparity would likely have been a good bit larger.

6. This living unit is defined as the disabled person, his or her spouse, and all children under 18 years of age.

7. A study of *recently* disabled individuals presents a pattern of income sources which is consistent with this pattern. Because the recently disabled have not likely achieved an "income source equilibrium," a somewhat higher proportion of their total income is accounted for by earnings than is the case for all of the disabled. See Frohlich (1975).

8. These numbers must be interpreted carefully. Because they refer to the income of the entire household in which the disabled person lives, the figures say little about the earnings of the disabled person. It is more likely that a spouse or other family member will be working in a household containing a disabled adult than in an identical household without the disability. Also, these comparisons are in terms of cash income differences, and hence exclude any differential effects from the receipt of in-kind benefits. During the 1970s the volume of in-kind benefits due to Food Stamps, Medicare, and Medicaid rose rapidly. Because of their low earnings and their categorical qualification for certain public assistance programs (notably, SSI), the disabled are likely to receive substantially more in-kind benefits per family unit than are the nondisabled. This would reduce the income disparity between the groups from that indicated in table 2.5.

9. In the United States, an income poverty line is set for several categories of families depending on family size and composition and rural-urban location. This set of poverty lines is based on budget studies and is adjusted over time by changes in the Consumer Price Index. A family is defined as being poor if its cash income falls below the poverty cut-off for families of that family's size, composition and location.

10. Such constraints can, in fact, be viewed as capital market imperfections, and as such they become yet another rationale for collective action.

11. The case for aiding the disabled stemming from this objective is no different from the case of assisting any poor person. Because disabled people have a far higher probability of being poor than other people, however, this issue is explicitly introduced here.

118

12. If workers and employers both had full information on the risks associated with various jobs of each employer, one would expect that the wage rates for risky jobs would, holding all else constant, be higher than that for safe jobs. In this case, employers would have incentives to undertake safety measures. That such full information is absent is clear.

13. Our discussion of "equal access" in this section draws heavily from Gliedman and Roth (1980).

Chapter 3

1. For a more complete discussion of the interrelationship between the insurance and welfare aspects of social security see Burkhauser and Warlick (1981).

2. The most recent of these is the National Commission on State Workers' Compensation Laws (1972). The commission's report contained eighty-four recommendations, nineteen of which were considered to be so essential that federal action was deemed necessary if states did not act voluntarily.

3. While these programs comprise the military-related cash income support programs for the disabled, there exist a wide range of other programs which provides health and other service to disabled veterans or their disabled dependents. Appendix A identifies several additional military-related programs with a total public expenditure cost for the disabled of over $4 billion.

4. See Berkowitz and Rubin (1977), p. 34.

5. U.S. Office of Management and Budget (1979).

6. This section was prepared with the assistance of Gregory Christiansen.

7. See Haveman (1979).

8. U.S. Office of Management and Budget (1979).

9. For several reasons, these calculations must be interpreted with caution. First, as noted earlier, some of the benefits may go to disabled persons who are above or below working age, and our adjustments to account for this are crude. Second, some of the benefits are paid to support the dependents of working-age disabled people. We have treated these as expenditures on behalf of the disabled. Finally, while we call these public expenditures, it is clear that a number of state and local programs on behalf of the disabled are not included in the total.

10. And it should be noted that in addition to the $70 billion of public expenditures on the disabled, there are another $50 billion of private expenditures (private insurance disability payments) on disabled people. The figures are adjusted from 1975 data in Berkowitz and Rubin (1977).

11. See U.S. Congressional Budget Office (1979) for a discussion of such issues concerning urban transportation for handicapped persons.

Chapter 4

1. Department of Health, Education, and Welfare, Social Security Administration [20 CFR Parts 404, 416] [Regulations No. 4, 16].

2. See Treitel (1979).

3. A child aged 18 or a child attending school and aged 21 who is receiving at least one-half of his or her income from his or her parents is considered a dependent child.

4. Van de Water's results are not evidence of a decrease in the number of beneficiaries receiving high benefits relative to earnings. His estimates use a worker's *highest* five years

119

out of his last ten years of work as the measure of earnings. He also does not consider the value of Medicare.

5. See Hambor (1975), Lando and Hopkins (1977), and Thompson and Van de Water (1976).

6. Because one can file a claim immediately upon disability-related unemployment, it is conceivable that no lag would be present. On the other hand, if the unemployed worker were to engage in a job search before applying, it would be appropriate to model the process with some lag.

7. The rate used by Lando and Hopkins (1977) is the value of new DI awards divided by average earnings for a worker with three dependents.

8. Bayo, Goss, and Weisman (1978) show that in 1977 the incidence of disability among male workers aged 50–54, 55–59, and 60–64 was 5, 9, and 12 times greater, respectively, than that of male workers aged 30–34. Thus, if the incidence remains constant across age groups, the number of disabled people will increase significantly in the first part of the twenty-first century due to this demographic change.

9. See Lando and Hopkins (1977).

10. See Lando and Krute (1976) and Howards and Brehm (1978).

11. It should be noted that the labor supply effects of the program are related to the growth of program expenditures and rolls discussed in chapter 3 and in the previous section. To the extent that the structure of disability programs induces an increase in decisions to apply or a reduction in decisions to leave, both of which relate to labor supply, the result will be an increase in the size of program expenditures and rolls.

The issue of the labor supply impacts of disability policy pertains to the entire set of programs targeted on disabled working-age persons. In this section, however, we discuss this issue in the context of the DI and SSI programs, because they are the dominant programs targeted on disabled workers.

12. See Luft (1978).

13. See Parsons (1980a) and Parsons (1980b).

14. See Leonard (1979).

15. DI recipients are permitted a trial work period of up to twelve months. During these months, unlimited earnings are permitted without loss of benefits. Once a DI recipient has worked twelve months (not necessarily consecutively) additional earnings above $300 per month are considered prima facia evidence of SGA and warrant loss of all DI benefits in the absence of controverting evidence.

16. In fact, the earning test may be more severe than stated in this example because DI recipients who earn between $180 and $300 per month may be considered capable of SGA, and their cases are subject to individual adjudication using all relevant medical and vocational evidence. Only those earning below $180 per month are presumed not capable of SGA.

17. In our hypothetical cases we use a single-year replacement rate as a measure of adequacy. A potentially superior measure is a life-time replacement rate. For instance, it can be argued that two workers, one with a constant age-earnings profile and the other with a rising age-earnings profile, but both with equal discounted life-time earnings, would be equally well off if they each received the same absolute DI benefit (an equivalent "wealth replacement ration"). But our single-year measure would show the second worker with a lower replacement rate. In addition, if adequacy is thought of in terms of replacing consumption, then a "wealth replacement rate" is more likely to measure this variable. Virtually all public policy discussion, however, is in terms of single-year replacement rates.

18. For a definition of the poverty line for families of two and four, see Plotnick and Skidmore (1975), pp. 31–46.

120

19. This strong conclusion rests on the proposition that in-kind benefits—Food Stamps and Medicare—have a cash equivalent value to recipients which should be included in income in calculating poverty. It needs to be tempered to the extent that the needs of disabled people may be greater than those of the nondisabled, say because of large medical expenses. Moreover, for any of the categories of recipients shown, there is a distribution of beneficiaries by income. For those in the bottom tail of the distribution, poverty status is more likely. While the 1972 Survey of Disabled Adults showed poverty rates of nineteen and forty percent for unmarried beneficiaries, this estimate occurred prior to the introduction of the SSI program and the rapid expansion of benefit levels and does not reflect the cash equivalent value of in-kind transfers.

20. The Social Security Administration critique of the study found methodological flaws in the GAO procedure. In a follow-up study, the SSA found less discrepancy both within and among states than is implied in the GAO study (Gallicchio and Bye, 1980). For files with complete information, this study found the probability of disagreement among examiners within a state to be 12 percent and the probability of disagreements across states to be 16 percent.

21. An actual field test by the Social Security Administration compared the SSI determination process in all states versus the process in the twenty-three states in which SSA does not administer state-designed supplements. It found that little, if any, greater uniformity in "administrative quality" would result from direct SSA control of SSI determination. See Sunshine (1979).

Chapter 5

1. An example of a financial evaluation study is that of the Beneficiticiary Rehabilitation Program (BRP), in which the Social Security Administration was enabled to expend an amount equal to 1.5 percent of Disability Insurance benefits for rehabilitation (Treitel, 1975). The study was a controversial one and was criticized by the General Accounting Office (1976), in part because of the narrow basis of the analysis, which focused only on the question of whether the program led to reductions in DI benefits in excess of program expenditures.

2. Many of these studies are reviewed in L. Kisner (1973).

3. Some of Conley's estimated ratios were substantially higher. For example, using a 4 percent discount rate, the ratio was 19 for 1958 data.

4. On the other hand, it is reasonable to hypothesize that the sociopsychological effects of disablement and earnings loss are greater for older than for younger workers, suggesting that efforts targeted at this group may be more efficient.

5. Levitan and Taggart (1977) present evidence on both of these effects. Slack labor markets are shown to affect strongly the employment status of disabled workers, especially the severely disabled. And the disincentive effects of income transfers are suggested as an explanation of the low employment effects of rehabilitation services provided to the severely disabled.

6. The discussion in this section relies heaviliy on Christiansen (1981).

7. This framework was developed by Haveman (1977) to evaluate the Netherlands Social Employment Program.

8. Direct benefits are defined as the value of output produced plus the increased productivity of the clients—benefit categories 1 and 2 in table 5.2.

Chapter 6

1. Burkhauser and Smeeding (1981) show that because SSI benefits are reduced dollar for dollar by the presence of OASI benefits, the redistributive aspects of OASI are lower for poor workers than for higher income workers. This is also the case for DI, whose benefits are also taxed at 100 percent.

2. While a private disability system based on pure insurance principles would also have some effect on work behavior, the effect would tend to be smaller. Such a program would not be likely to rely on nonhealth-related criteria for eligibility and would not be likely to provide as generous a replacement of earnings.

3. Currently benefits are reduced by 5/9 of 1 percent for each month they are taken prior to age 65, so that at age 62 (the earliest possible age of acceptance) yearly benefits are reduced by 20 percent. The 1981 proposals will reduce benefits by 1¼ percent or by 45 percent at age 62.

4. That by Representative Pickle, chairman of the Subcommittee on Social Security.

References

Allan, Kathryn H. "First Findings of the 1972 Survey of the Disabled: General Characteristics." *Social Security Bulletin*, October 1976, pp. 18–37.

Bayo, Francisco; Goss, Stephen; and Weisman, Samuel. *Experience of Disabled Worker Benefits under OASDI, 1972–1976.* U.S. Department of Health, Education, and Welfare, Social Security Administration, Actuarial Study no. 75, Publication no. (SSA) 78–11525, June 1978.

Bellante, Donald M. "A Multivariate Analysis of a Vocational Rehabilitation Program." *Journal of Human Resources*, Spring 1972, pp. 226–41.

Berkowitz, Monroe, and Dean, David. "Medical Care Costs of Disabled Persons." Mimeographed. Department of Economics, Rutgers University, June 1980.

———. "An Evaluation of the Structure and Functions of Disability Programs." Mimeographed. Bureau of Economic Research, Rutgers University, June 1975.

Berkowitz, Monroe, and Rubin, Jeffrey. "The Costs of Disability: Estimates of Program Expenditures for Disability, 1969–1975." Mimeographed. Bureau of Economic Research, Rutgers University, August 1977.

Bishop, J., and Haveman, R. "Selective Employment Subsidies: Can Okun's Law Be Repealed?" *American Economic Review*, 1979, pp. 124–30.

Borus, M., and Hamermesh, D. "Study of the Net Employment Effects of Public Service Employment-Econometric Analyses." In *Job Creation through Public Service Employment*, An Interim Report to the Congress of the National Commission for Manpower Policy, 3:89–150. Commissioned Papers. Washington, D.C.: National Commission for Manpower Policy, 1978.

Burkhauser, Richard, and Smeeding, Timothy. "The Net Impact of the Social Security System on the Poor." *Public Policy* 29, no. 2 (Spring 1981).

Burkhauser, Richard V., and Warlick, Jennifer L. "Disentangling the Annuity from the Redistributive Aspects of the Social Security." *Review of Income and Wealth*, December 1981.

Chamber of Commerce of the United States. *Analysis of Workmen's Compensation Laws, 1978.* Washington, D.C.: Chamber of Commerce of the United States, 1968.

————. *Analysis of Workers' Compensation Laws, 1979.* Washington, D.C.: Chamber of Commerce of the United States, 1979.

Christiansen, Gregory B. "Sheltered Workshops as a Means of Benefiting the Disabled." Ph.D. dissertation, University of Wisconsin, 1981.

Conley, Ronald W. *The Economics of Vocational Rehabilitation.* Baltimore: The Johns Hopkins University Press, 1965.

————. "A Benefit-Cost Analysis of the Vocational Rehabilitation Program." *Journal of Human Resources*, Spring 1969, pp. 226–52.

Conley, Ronald W., and Noble, J., Jr. "Workmen's Compensation Reform Changes for the 1980s." *American Rehabilitation*, January–February 1973.

Derthick, Martha. *Policymaking for Social Security.* Washington, D.C.: The Brookings Institution, 1979.

Franklin, Paula. "Impact of Substantial Gainful Activity Level on Disabled Beneficiary Work Patterns." *Social Security Bulletin*, August 1976, pp. 20–29.

Frolich, Philip. "Income of the Newly Disabled: Survey of Recently Disabled Adults." *Social Security Bulletin*, September 1975, pp. 3–18.

Gallicchio, Sal, and Bye, Barry. *Consistency of Initial Disability Decisions among and within States.* U.S. Department of Health and Human Services, Social Security Administration, Office of Policy, Office of Research and Statistics, Staff Paper no. 39, Publication no. 13–11869, July 1980.

Garrad, J. "Impairment and Disability: Their Measurement, Prevalence, and Psychological Cost." In *Impairment, Disability, and Handicap*, ed. Dennis Lees and Stella Shaw. London: Heineman, 1974.

Gliedman, John, and Roth, William. *The Unexpected Minority.* New York: Harcourt, Brace, and Jovanovich, 1980.

Greenleigh Associates. *The Role of the Sheltered Workshops in the Rehabilitation of the Severely Handicapped.* New York: Greenleigh Associates, 1976.

Hambor, John C. *Unemployment and Disability: An Economic Analysis with Time Series Data.* U.S. Department of Health, Education, and Welfare, Social Security Administration, Office of Research and Statistics, Staff Paper no. 20, January 1975.

Haveman, Robert H. "Direct Job Creation: Potentials and Realities." University of Wisconsin at Madison, Institute for Research on Poverty, Discussion Paper 570–79, September 1979.

REFERENCES

————. "A Benefit-Cost and Policy Analysis of the Netherlands' Social Employment System." Mimeographed. University of Leiden, 1977.

Hodgens, Evan. "Key Changes in Major Pension Plans." *Monthly Labor Review,* July 1975, pp. 22–27.

Howards, Irving, and Brehm, Henry. "The Impossible Dream: The Nationalization of Welfare? A Look at Disability Insurance and State Influence over Federal Government." *Polity* 11, no. 1 (Fall 1978): 7–26.

Johnson, G., and Tomola, J. "The Fiscal Substitution Effect of Alternative Approaches to Public Service Employment Policy." *Journal of Human Resources,* Winter 1977, pp. 3–26.

Johnson, William; Cullinan, Paul; and Curington, William. "The Adequacy of Workers' Compensation Benefits." Syracuse University, The Maxwell School, Health Studies Program no. 33, February 1978.

Kisner, L. *A Review of Benefit-Cost Analysis in Vocational Rehabilitation.* Supplemental Studies for the National Commission on State Workman's Compensation Laws. Washington, D.C.: GPO, 1973.

Koitz, David. *Current Legislative Issues in the Social Security Disability Insurance Programs.* U.S. Department of Health, Education, and Welfare, ASMB, Staff Report, April 1977.

Ladinsky, Jack. "Viet Nam, the Veterans, and the Veterans Administration." University of Wisconsin at Madison, Institute for Research on Poverty, Reprint 221, 1977.

Lando, Mordechai E. "The Interaction between Health and Education." *Social Security Bulletin,* December 1975, pp. 16–23.

Lando, Mordechai E., and Hopkins, Timothy R. "Modeling Applications for Disability Insurance." Conference Paper for the American Economic Association Meetings, December 1977.

Lando, Mordechai E., and Krute, Aaron. "Disability Insurance: Program Issues and Research." *Social Security Bulletin,* October 1976, pp. 3–17.

Lawrence, W.J., and Leeds, S. *An Inventory of Federal Income Transfer Programs, Fiscal Year 1977.* White Plains, N.Y.: Institute for Socio-Economic Studies, 1978.

Leonard, Jonathan. "The Social Security Disability Program and Labor Force Participation." National Bureau of Economic Research Working Paper 392, 1979.

Levitan, S. A., and Taggart, R. *Jobs for the Disabled.* Baltimore: The Johns Hopkins University Press, 1977.

Luft, Harold. *Poverty and Health.* Cambridge: Ballinger Publishing, 1978.

McMillan, Alma W., and Bixby, Ann Kallman. "Social Welfare Expenditures, Fiscal Year 1978," *Social Security Bulletin,* May 1980, pp. 3–17.

Muller, L. Scott. "Receipt of Multiple Benefits by Disabled Worker Benefi-

125

ciaries." U.S. Department of Health, Education, and Welfare, Social Security Administration, Office of Research and Statistics, Office of Policy, Working Paper Series no. 15, May 1980.

Nagi, Saad. "The Concept and Measurement of Disability." In *Disability Policies and Government Policies*, ed. E. Berkowitz. New York: Praeger Publishers, 1979.

Oi, Walter. "The Impact of Disability on Full Income." Conference Paper for the American Economic Association Meetings, August 1978.

———. "The Impact of Disability on Full Income." Mimeographed, 1977.

Parsons, Donald O. "The Decline in Male Labor Force Participation." *Journal of Political Economy* 88, no. 1 (February 1980a): 117–34.

———. "The Male Labor Force Decision: Health, Reported Health, and Economic Incentives." Mimeographed, 1980b.

Perloff, J. M., and Wachter, M. L. "The New Jobs Tax Credit: An Evaluation of the 1977–78 Wage Subsidy Program." *American Economic Review*, 1979, pp. 173–79.

Plotnick, Robert B., and Skidmore, Felicity. *Progress against Poverty.* New York: Academic Press, 1975.

Price, Daniel. "Workers' Compensation Programs in the 1970s." *Social Security Bulletin*, May 1979, pp. 3–24.

The Report of the National Commission on State Workers' Compensation Laws. Washington, D.C.: GPO, July 1972.

Riley, Lawrence E., and Nagi, Saad Z., eds. *Disability in the United States: A Compendium of Data on Prevalence and Programs.* Columbus, Ohio: Division of Disability Research, Department of Physical Medicine, The Ohio State University, 1970.

Sunshine, Jonathan. *Disability.* Office of Management and Budget Staff Technical Paper, 1979.

Thompson, Lawrence H., and Van der Water, Paul N. *The Short-Run Behavior of the Social Security Trust Funds.* U.S. Department of Health, Education, and Welfare, ISP–ASPE, Technical Staff Analysis Paper no. 8, July 1976.

Treitel, Ralph. "Effects of Financing Disabled-Beneficiary Rehabilitation." *Social Security Bulletin,* November 1975, pp. 16–18.

———. *Disability Claimants Who Contest Denials and Win Reversals through Hearings.* U.S. Department of Health, Education, and Welfare, Social Security Administration, Office of Research and Statistics, Office of Policy, Working Paper Series no. 3, February 1979.

U.S. Congressional Budget Office. *Urban Transportation for Handicapped Persons: Alternative Federal Approaches.* Budget Issue Paper for Fiscal Year 1981, November 1979.

U.S. Department of Commerce, Bureau of Census (DOL, BC). *1970 Census of Population: Persons with Work Disability*, PC (2)–6C. Washington, D.C.: GPO, January 1973.

U.S. Department of Health, Education, and Welfare, Social and Rehabilitation Services. "Old-Age Assistance, Aid to the Blind, and Aid to Permanently and Totally Disabled: Report on Monthly Cost Standards," Form SRS-1971. Washington, D.C.: GPO, 1968a.

———. "State Maximums and Other Methods of Limiting Money Payments to Recipients of the Special Types of Public Assistance." National Center for Social Statistics Report D-3 (10/68). Washington, D.C.: GPO, 1968b.

———. "Supplementary Security Income for the Aged, Blind, and Disabled: Summary of State Payment Levels, and Medicaid Decisions," ISS-12-100. Washington, D.C.: GPO, 1977.

U.S. Department of Health, Education, and Welfare, Social Security Administration. *A Guide to Supplemental Security Income.* Washington, D.C.: GPO, 1978a.

———. *History of the Provisions of Old-Age, Survivors, Disability, and Health Insurance, 1935–77.* Washington, D.C.: GPO, 1978b.

———. "How the Disabled Fare in the Labor Market." *Monthly Labor Review*, September 1980a, pp. 48–52.

———. *If You Become Disabled.* Washington, D.C.: G.P.O, 1978c.

———. *Social Security Bulletin*, May 1979a.

———. *Social Security Bulletin*, June 1979b.

———. *Social Security Bulletin*, July 1979c.

———. *Social Security Bulletin, Annual Statistical Supplement, 1975.* Washington, D.C.: GPO, 1977.

———. *Social Security Bulletin, Annual Statistical Supplement, 1976.* Washington, D.C.: GPO, 1980b.

U.S. Department of Health and Human Services, Social Security Administration. *Social Security Bulletin*, February 1981a.

———. *Social Security Bulletin, Annual Statistical Supplement, 1977–1979.* Washington, D.C.: GPO, 1981b.

U.S. Department of Labor, Bureau of Labor Statistics. *Employment and Earnings.* Washington, D.C.: GPO, January 1970.

———. *Employment and Earnings.* Washington, D.C.: GPO, January 1979a.

———. *Handbook of Labor Statistics, 1975.* Washington, D.C.: GPO, 1975.

———. *Monthly Labor Review.* Vol. 102, no. 7. Washington, D.C.: GPO, 1979b.

U.S. General Accounting Office. *Report to the Congress: The Social Security Administration Should Provide More Management and Leadership in Determining Who Is Eligible for Disability Benefits.* HRD-76-105. 1976.

U.S. Office of Management and Budget. *The Budget of the United States*

Government: Fiscal Year 1980. Washington, D.C.: GPO, 1979.

Van de Water, Paul N. "Disability Insurance." Conference paper for the Annual Meetings of the American Economic Association, August 1978.

Worrall, John D. "A Benefit-Cost Analysis of the Vocational Rehabilitation Program." *Journal of Human Resources*, Spring 1978, pp. 285–98.

Index

67–70; effectiveness of, 67–71; productivity of workers in, 70–71; public expenditures on, 67

Replacement rates, 3, 6, 43, 44, 47–48, 55–62, 97

Roosevelt (President), 41

"Safety net," 57, 62, 65, 90, 91

Sheltered workshops, 34, 66, 71–74; administration of, 34, 71–72; benefit-cost analyses of, 72–74; for blind, 73; effectiveness of, 71–74; growth of, 35; for mentally retarded, 73; public expenditure for, 35, 72

Social Security Act and disabled persons, 40–41, 90

Social Security Administration surveys, 8, 9, 17, 51, 53

Social Security Disability Insurance. *See* Disability insurance.

Substantial Gainful Activity (SGA), 28, 41, 46, 49, 54, 99, 106–13

Supplemental Security Income (SSI), 4, 29–30, 48, 54, 56–57, 60–65, 71, 89–97; appeal and judicial review for, 107; financing of, 113; integration of with other programs, 110–11; population served by, and growth, 108–9; program expenditures, 30, 31, 109–10; termination of, 112

Targeted Jobs Tax Credit (TJTC), 36–37, 76–77, 80, 98

Transbus controversy, 83–84

Truman (President), 41

Veterans Compensation and Pension programs, 4, 32, 90; benefits of, 32; eligibility for, 32, 106–7; financing of, 113; integration of, with other programs, 110–11; population of, and growth, 108–9; program expenditures, 31, 109–10, termination of, 112

Vocational Rehabilitation Act of 1921, 35

Vocational rehabilitation programs, 33, 61, 97; participation in, 33; program expenditure for, 31

Workers' Compensation, 4, 30, 56–57, 60–64, 90; eligibility for, 30, 106–7; financing of, 113; integration of, with other programs, 110–11; population served by, and growth, 108–9; program expenditures for, 31, 109–10; termination of, 112